Classic

SAN FRANCISCO

From Ocean Beach to Mission Bay

Classic

SAN FRANCISCO

From Ocean Beach to Mission Bay

FRANK DUNNIGAN

THE
History
PRESS

Published by The History Press
Charleston, SC
www.historypress.net

First published 2019

Title page: Vintage 1904 streetlight in front of the St. Francis Hotel, Union Square, 2019. *Dwayne Ratleff photo.*

Opposite: Lighted archway for Grand Army of the Republic gathering, 3rd and Market Streets looking east, 1903. *OpenSFHistory.*

Manufactured in the United States

ISBN 9781467141604

Library of Congress Control Number: 2019943362

Long ago, far away,
Life was clear,
Close your eyes.
Remember…is a place from long ago…

—Harry Nilsson (1941–1994)

Vintage postcard of Cliff House and California poppies, circa 1900. *Glenn D. Koch collection.*

Contents

Old and new San Francisco come together on Market Street near 4th Street, looking west, in 2017. *Michael Fraley photo.*

Acknowledgements

T he author is grateful to the following individuals and organizations for their generous contributions of photos, stories and fact-checking over many years. Most importantly, profound thanks to all for ongoing support and encouragement toward the development of this book.

Tammy Aramian
Artam Photography
Elizabeth Ashcroft
Al Barna
James Battaglieri
Alan J. Canterbury
Bob Carini
Carnaval San Francisco
Kevin Carroll
Chinese Culture Center
Carlos Cordonero
Caroline Culler
Alice McDonald Dieden
Dllu Photography
Marc and Vicki Duffett
Dunnigan Family
Emiliano Echeverria
Frank Florianz

Rogelio Foronda
Michael Fraley
John Freeman
Scott Frischer
Claire Mibach Fugate
Fullmetal Photography
David Gallagher
Robin Galante
Andrew Galvan
Vivian Gisin
Doris Goodwin
Tom Gray
Victor Grigas
Clare Harper
Alvis Hendley
Anne Evers Hitz
Judy Hitzeman
Randall Ann Homan

Bernadette Hooper
George and Catherine Horsfall
Paul Judge
Christine Meagher Keller
Max Kirkeberg
Glenn D. Koch
Laurie Krill
Nancy Ann Kuhn
Woody LaBounty
Lick-Wilmerding High School
Paul Martin
John Martini
Metropolitan Transportation Agency
Mission Dolores Archives
Noe Hill
OpenSFHistory
Mike Oria
Parkmerced Vision
Duane Ratleff
Mary Ellen (MER) Ring
Sherrie Katz Rosenberg
Richard Rothman
Bernadette Ruane
San Francisco Heritage
San Francisco History Association

San Francisco History Days
San Francisco Italian Athletic Club
San Francisco Public Library
Eleanor Sananman
Dave Schweisguth
Alice Ho Seher
David Seibold
Robert Skelton Photography
Judy Skelton
SFNeon.org
Bob and Carolyn Ross
James R. Smith
Sullivan Family
Adam Susaneck
Jeff Thomas
Jack Tillmany
Paul Totah
Alfred Twu
Lorri Ungaretti
Michael Van Dyke
Westerhouse Family
Western Neighborhoods Project
Wikimedia Commons
Wolfman SF Photography
Marco Zanoli

Introduction

Since at least the 1700s, multiple writers have made reference to the inevitability of both death and taxes. To these might be added a third inescapable certainty: CHANGE.

During the Gold Rush era, from 1849 to 1851, San Francisco suffered seven devastating fires, each of them consuming large portions of the fledgling city. The worst of these took place in May 1851, when it was estimated that two thousand buildings—75 percent of the local structures—had been destroyed. As each rebuilding effort was completed, residents often felt that a brand new city had been created from the ashes.

Those disasters pale in comparison to the losses from the earthquake and fire of 1906. San Francisco–born author Jack London, then thirty years old, stated categorically:

> *Not in history has a modern imperial city been so completely destroyed. San Francisco is gone.*

When San Francisco celebrated the Portola Festival in 1909, it was a declaration that the City had recovered from the devastation of the 1906 disasters. Many argued at the time that it was an entirely different place, with only a few throwbacks to its earlier days.

Likewise, the Panama-Pacific International Exposition in 1915 provided further reassurance that San Francisco had fully emerged from the shadow of disaster and was moving forward. New housing developments of the

Aerial view of Market Street, 1926. The most prominent downtown building at the time was the then-new Pacific Telephone & Telegraph Building, located at 140 New Montgomery Street (top center), which was San Francisco's tallest office tower until 1964. At the time, many more Financial District skyscrapers, plus the Golden Gate and Bay Bridges, existed only in the minds of architects and engineers. *OpenSFHistory.*

time, ranging from St. Francis Wood to the Excelsior, were often regarded as a wonder to old-timers, with the automobile beginning to contribute significantly to the City's rebirth and expansion. The City's business district once again became the center for financial transactions west of the Mississippi River.

During the financial boom times of the 1920s, new skyscrapers were built, changing the character of the downtown area and creating thousands of new jobs in the construction, banking, insurance and utilities industries. Grand movie palaces sprang up along Market Street, Mission Street and into outlying areas, bringing new technology to the masses. Housing was in demand, and thousands of new homes and apartment buildings were constructed in every neighborhood.

However, during the period from 1930 to 1940, San Francisco's population remained absolutely flat, with U.S. Census Bureau figures showing growth from 634,394 to 634,596—a net gain of only 202 residents in that entire decade. Things were about to drastically change again.

In the World War II years, San Francisco began growing significantly. Local businesses went into high gear producing the materials needed during the global conflict. Many factories and shipyards operated 24/7, with employees working first, second and third shifts. Movie houses and restaurants also operated around the clock, catering to the needs of workers for meals and entertainment during their off-hours. During the 1940s, San Francisco's population jumped from 634,536 to 775,357—an increase of more than 22 percent in just ten years.

In the postwar years, residents saw new homes and businesses rapidly sprouting up in central locations that had been vacated after the removal of a cluster of cemeteries. In the Oceanview, Merced Heights and Ingleside neighborhoods (collectively known as OMI), along with the sand dunes and former cabbage fields of the Sunset, Parkmerced and Stonestown areas, housing was expanding rapidly, stretching all the way to the Pacific Ocean. By the 1950s, old Victorian homes were falling in the Western Addition and being replaced with high-rises, and soon, streets were being carved into hillsides for brand-new developments in the Twin Peaks and Diamond Heights areas.

The suburban growth that began in the 1950s caused San Francisco's population to drop for each of the next several decades—from 1960 until the dawn of the 1990s—but residents still found themselves startled by many of the changes that were emerging: freeways, downtown auto congestion, overcrowded schools resulting from the postwar baby boom and the rising cost of housing due to inflation. By 1980, many modest San Francisco homes were beginning to sell for upward of $100,000, and longtime residents were shocked.

Today, San Francisco is surely involved in yet another transformative era of change. No one—current resident or interested former resident—has the least bit of doubt over this.

Looking back, many people point a finger at changes that have occurred since the turn of the millennium as the beginning of the present wave of change. There certainly were some dramatic shifts that have been causing global change since well before the year 2000:

- The rise of the Internet and personal computing devices
- The online presence of virtually every type of organization
- Changing business models involving customer interactions
- The shift of many manufacturing operations to lower-cost locales
- Increasing inflation impacting the cost of living

There were several additional factors that caused specific impacts on lives and businesses in the San Francisco Bay area:

- The decline in rail travel and freight transport
- The shift of most shipping operations to the Port of Oakland
- Corporate headquarters moving outside San Francisco
- The closure of numerous local U.S. military bases
- Fewer children living in San Francisco

All of these changes set into motion a series of other events, much like the ripples that result from a rock being thrown into a calm body of water and radiate outward for some time after the rock is thrown.

Shifting employment patterns caused job losses for tens of thousands of workers, with many individuals choosing to relocate to another area as their own personal best course of action. In some cases, new tracts of land opened up after the demolition of old businesses, causing much discussion about possible uses. Transportation systems were challenged, with passenger loads at the breaking point during more than just the traditional morning and afternoon rush hours. All of these issues have been simmering for decades.

Meanwhile, a building boom created dozens of new high-rise office towers and apartment/condo buildings of all sizes, primarily along the City's eastern side—South-of-Market, Mission Bay (on land that was formerly railroad tracks and warehouses), Hunters Point (on and adjacent to the grounds of the old Naval Shipyard, which closed in 1994), the Bayview District site of the old Candlestick Park (torn down in 2015) and the grounds of Treasure Island, another former U.S. Navy facility (after it served as a World's Fair site in 1939–40), which was given back to the City by the federal government in 1997. Many new residents were attracted to the area because of these developments—another factor that has been in place since the local population increased between 1980 and 1990 after having been in decline since 1960.

At the same time, San Francisco's population has been condensed, age-wise. The number of children has drastically declined since before the turn of the millennium, leading to the easily verifiable statistic that "San Francisco has more dogs than kids." This massive population shift has impacted schools, retailers, houses of worship, the number of at-home parents, public transit ridership, and so forth. At the same time, many older residents are being priced out of housing—or, conversely, they have greatly profited from the increase in home values and are cashing out and relocating to less costly places, often out of state. This, too, has brought significant change to the lives of many people.

Many other aspects of daily life are also poised for change. Numerous Catholic elementary and high schools have closed in this millennium (based on the decline in the numbers of children living in San Francisco as well as other factors), with the buildings then leased to private institutions that are run by others. There has been increasing flight of the City's African American middle class, as their overall representation in the population has dropped from 13 percent to barely 6 percent in recent years. Certain Catholic churches in the Mission District (St. Peter, St. Anthony, St. Charles) are now part of a "Collaborative of Mission Parishes"—a concept which may well be extended to other areas in the future in order to allow for sharing of scarce staffing and financial resources. *Beach Blanket Babylon*, the widely popular stage revue in operation since 1974, announced in April 2019 that the final curtain will fall on December 31, 2019. The picturesque corkscrew turns of Lombard Street between Hyde and Leavenworth Streets are under consideration by civic leaders for the imposition of a new roadway toll for motorists. Some local politicians have even begun questioning the intrinsic value of the historic 1941 Cow Palace, just over the county line in Daly City, suggesting that the building might be demolished and the land turned over to other uses, such as housing and retail.

Today, many people complain that "the City has changed"—the implication being that all the old and familiar touchstones of their lives have been swept away overnight; clearly, such changes did not come about that quickly. The local landscape has been changing in thousands of tiny, subtle ways one little thread at a time, year after year, until a brand-new tapestry has been woven. Even the San Francisco that exists today will continue to change—bit by bit and day by day, in a never-ending process of evolution—into a place that exists just around the bend and is drastically different from its previous incarnation.

As local cable car conductors have been saying since 1873, "Look out for the curve!"

The Native Sons' Monument, also known as the Admission Day Monument, was dedicated in 1897—some forty-seven years after California achieved statehood. *Glenn D. Koch collection.*

1

Out for a Walk

As a veteran San Francisco walker (having first pounded the pavement between my parents' home at 18th Avenue and Vicente Street and the shopping areas of Taraval Street and West Portal Avenue back in the early 1950s with a then-non-driving mom), it's always interesting to me to see how things change. Until recently, the City and County of San Francisco did little more than install concrete sidewalks and asphalt pavement, perhaps with an occasional playground drinking fountain, rare bus shelter (at Junipero Serra Boulevard and Ocean Avenue, for example) or wooden benches painted forest green along Sunset Boulevard. Today, however, municipal government has provided a vast stockpile of new amenities available for the enjoyment of walkers.

ACTIVATING STREET SPACE

Merchandise displays, outdoor café and restaurant seating, street fairs and block parties, parklets and street vendors

Parklets: These amenities began to appear around 2011 in locations such as 3rd and Clement, 37th and Balboa, and along some of the retail portions of Judah, Noriega and Taraval Streets. Thanks to this transformation of a small number of curbside parking spaces with minimal construction, many neighborhoods now have additional public seating and container plantings that can be enjoyed by everyone and encourage pedestrian rather than car traffic in neighborhood shopping areas. These spots are often located adjacent to bakeries, delis and coffeehouses, thus creating a bit of a neighborhood social center while still ensuring quick turnover, as there are generally benches but no tables. Many merchants thoughtfully provide large water bowls for four-legged visitors.

Café and Restaurant Seating: Depending on the width of the sidewalk, established food service businesses may apply for permission to place their own tables and chairs on the sidewalk adjacent to the business for their customers' exclusive use.

Street Vendors: Individual vendors may apply for permission to sell food or other goods from mobile carts on public streets.

Street Fairs and Block Parties: Popular since the late 1960s, street fairs continue to enjoy support in many neighborhoods. Individual residents may also join together to request temporary use of a City street for informal gatherings. These temporary street closings (mysteriously called "street openings" in City-speak) can accommodate large regional events or smaller neighborhood block parties.

Merchandise Displays: Sidewalk displays of merchandise (often produce or books) can enliven a neighborhood walk. City officials monitor such displays to make sure they do not overwhelm available sidewalk space or cause unnecessary congestion.

Greening/Stormwater Management

Median plantings, street trees, sidewalk landscaping, parking lane planters, permeable pavement and more

Medians: The center divides on major streets, officially known as "medians," have changed considerably in recent years, some for the better and some…well, let's just say that the City and County of San Francisco have produced mixed results on this one. One area that has been vastly improved in recent times is 19th Avenue from Lincoln Way to Sloat Boulevard. Ever since the street was widened in 1940, this stretch of California Highway 1 has been a long, dismal six-lane stretch of concrete and asphalt. It was vastly improved in 2014, when the median was planted with a variety of small, hardy plantings designed to resist motor vehicle exhaust and survive with minimal maintenance. It's not exactly a

More utilities are being relocated underground, with new street lighting, additional trees and seating being added to neighborhood streets. Corner of 21st and Dolores Streets looking north, 2004 (*top*) and 2011 (*bottom*). *Max Kirkeberg collection.*

scenic parkway, but those plantings provide a softening effect and are a vast improvement upon the plain concrete center islands that were once home to various bits of litter and lost hubcaps. On the other hand, Sunset Boulevard from Lincoln Way to Sloat Boulevard presents a mixed bag of results. Since the 1930s, this street has been a grassy, tree-lined parkway, and its entire length was upgraded about forty years ago with new lawns and automated sprinklers. In fact, when there was a proposal around 1975 to route a new MUNI streetcar line along the Sunset Boulevard median, there was a huge neighborhood outcry of protest claiming that the plan would destroy the freshly renovated landscaping. By 2010, that 1970s landscape was looking pretty sad—the lawns were dead and weed-infested, with many of the older trees (planted by WPA crews in the 1930s) beginning to topple over with alarming frequency. A new variety of grass, claimed to be both drought-tolerant and low-maintenance, was installed to replace the dead grass. In less than a year, though, neighborhood complaints increased as the newly planted grass began looking worse than what it had replaced. The City then ripped it out and began to replant the median with a variety of plantings, some of which look more attractive than others, though weed control still seems to be something of a challenge. Dead and dying trees are sporadically being replaced—a project that might best have commenced in earnest twenty or thirty years ago.

Street Trees: The greening of San Francisco began in the 1960s with small street trees, many of which were planted by Friends of the Urban Forest and located around neighborhood shopping areas such as West Portal Avenue. Unfortunately, some of the plant choices made in those early days included some varieties that were not particularly well suited to sidewalk planting areas. Trees with invasive roots led to unfortunate long-term results, and other trees were allowed to grow to second-floor and higher elevations, diminishing the architectural effect of bay windows that were intended to bring in more daylight. As some of these trees begin to exceed thirty and forty years of age, there has been renewed discussion about long-term maintenance issues; although the City was involved in planting great numbers of them in the past, responsibility for the trees was eventually assigned to individual property owners.

PEDESTRIAN SAFETY/TRAFFIC CALMING

Crosswalks, curb ramps, bulb-outs, chicanes, medians/islands,
speed humps and traffic circles

Pedestrian Refuge Islands: Most of Noriega Street is an extra-wide thoroughfare that was laid out in a way that would accommodate a streetcar line that was never built (public transit on Noriega has always involved MUNI bus service), so this area has long posed a challenge to pedestrians. Crossing from one side to the other, especially in the busy retail areas clustered between 20th Avenue and Sunset Boulevard, has long been especially dangerous. Around 2011, the City began to address this problem by installing what are known as "pedestrian refuge islands" at many of the intersections. These allow pedestrians to safely pause at the midpoint of the crosswalk when navigating such a wide thoroughfare. Each of the small islands has been planted with native grasses and other drought-tolerant plantings. Overall, the project along Noriega Street has been a big improvement in terms of both visual effect and traffic safety.

Bulb-Outs/Curb Extensions: These designs continue the sidewalk into the parking lane and beyond to the street. This shortens the distance between opposite sides of the intersection, and pedestrians are able to cross quicker while remaining highly visible to oncoming traffic. Depending on a particular street's configuration, some bulb-outs also provide space for landscaping, street trees, benches, trash receptacles and other amenities. Generally located near corners, bulb-outs seldom require the loss of any on-street parking spaces.

Parking Lane Planters: Removing a single parking space and extending the sidewalk with a five-foot stretch of landscaped space allows for a visual narrowing of the roadway, which has the much desired effect of slowing down traffic to a speed that is safe for pedestrians in neighborhood shopping areas.

Chicanes: A chicane involves multiple midblock islands or curb extensions that are designed to force vehicle traffic into a weaving pattern rather than a straight line, thus discouraging motorists from speeding on residential streets. These installations are often difficult to implement, since the City is careful to avoid such installations on streets with MUNI lines or in areas near hospitals that receive regular ambulance traffic. Overall, chicanes are loved by some residents and despised by others. Rather ironically, the word "chicane" comes from the French word *chicaner*, which means "to quibble."

Sidewalk bulb-out with a mosaic neighborhood shopping district sign designed by Colette Crutcher, 39th Avenue and Balboa Street, 2016. *Dave Schweisguth image.*

Speed Humps: No longer called "bumps" since the effect has been slightly diminished to prevent possible damage to vehicles and passengers, speed humps are generally installed by the City in response to neighborhood requests for help with slowing traffic through residential areas. Speed humps are practical only on streets with fewer than six thousand vehicles per day.

Traffic Circles: These are likely the most controversial of all street projects, although San Franciscans, especially in the Western Neighborhoods, have long understood the concept—think of the St. Francis Wood intersection at Santa Ana Way and St. Francis Boulevard, with the massive fountain that was often filled with bubbles from dishwashing liquid. Most people know how to navigate around this intersection, but when similar circles have been installed elsewhere in the City, motorists have demonstrated confusion, anger and sometimes just plain poor judgement.

Reclaiming Roadway Space

*On-street bicycle parking, living alleys
and pedestrian-only streets/alleys*

Living Alleys: These are generally complex projects that often limit motor vehicles but do not ban them outright. Maiden Lane off Union Square is a classic example that has been in place for more than fifty years, with limited hours for vehicle access followed by conversion for several hours to a pedestrian-only environment. Living alleys often involve various combinations of streetscape elements such as special sidewalk paving, distinctive street lighting, benches and café/restaurant seating.

Bicycle Parking: Rather than restricting pedestrian access to limited sidewalk space with the installation of bike racks, an alternate solution has been to convert a single curbside parking space to bicycles-only parking by bolting a metal bike rack to the street and protecting the space from vehicle damage/intrusion by installing sturdy planter boxes on each end.

Other Streetscape Elements

*New items include special sidewalk paving, street lighting, seating,
banners, informational kiosks, fixed pedestal news racks, public art,
public toilets, transit shelters, trash cans and the like*

Lighting: City government maintains an extensive catalog of different types of street lighting. The "Path of Gold" three-lamp fixtures on Market Street are unique to their setting, as are the similar but smaller two-lamp fixtures on downtown commercial streets in the Union Square area. Many individual neighborhoods are now working with the City to replace the harsh mercury vapor streetlights that were widely used in the 1960s with smaller fixtures more suited to providing greater sidewalk illumination for pedestrians.

Banners: Banners lend a festive air to commercial strips and major thoroughfares like 19th Avenue. Often used to advertise events (de Young Museum exhibitions, Fleet Week, etc.), they are also available to public and private organizations to advertise their own events (Lowell High School's fifty years at its Lake Merced campus in 2013, the 150th anniversary of St. Ignatius in 2005). Sponsors pay the City a fee for a monthlong display of such banners.

Art: Artwork in public places has long been a part of the San Francisco street scene. From vintage pre-1906 pieces to contemporary works such as *Cupid's Span*, a sixty-foot-tall red-tipped bow and arrow installed in a grassy park setting on the Embarcadero in 2002, public art enriches the lives of everyone.

Water: One of the newest sidewalk amenities, water-bottle refill stations provide a tremendous convenience but without the sanitary concerns or maintenance costs of drinking fountains. The program began in 2010, and there are now more than thirty-six refill stations on the streets of San Francisco, plus additional spots on the grounds of many public schools.

Water-bottle filling station adjacent to a Richmond District parklet in 2016. *Western Neighborhoods Project.*

Restrooms: As any walker will attest, this is an essential public service.

While there is always some disagreement about certain aspects of City life, it is generally accepted that most of our neighborhoods have become far more pedestrian-friendly in recent times with these newer streetscape elements.

Fox Theatre, circa 1944. *Jack Tillmany collection.*

2
Buttered Popcorn Days

Until the 1960s, San Francisco residents knew that they were living in a movie-loving town, with many entertainment choices:

- Several big downtown theatres with first-run films
- Many first-/second-run neighborhood locations
- Third-run houses with offerings that frequently changed
- Small independent theatres with international/art films and newsreels
- Drive-ins

After World War II, television began to present a serious challenge to the movie industry. As the number of U.S. households with television sets grew from below 1 percent in 1946 to more than 55 percent in 1954 and more than 90 percent by 1962, many people were quietly transitioning from moviegoers to couch potatoes. The baby boom also kept many once-avid movie fans at home with children in the evenings monitoring homework, bath times and bedtimes.

By the early 1960s, San Francisco theatres were experiencing serious declines in ticket sales. These are the locations—now long gone—that were once popular spots for local residents to "dress up" for a night out.

Fox: The biggest and grandest of all was the Fox, a $5 million architectural extravaganza containing 4,650 seats, which opened at 1350 Market Street in June 1929, when Hollywood glitz was at an all-time high. Original plans for the largest theatre west of the Mississippi also called for a one-thousand-room hotel to be built adjacent to and above the ornate theatre. However, a multimillion dollar cost overrun (to deal with a previously unknown river flowing beneath the building site) led to the demise of those plans. The stock market crash in October 1929 brought serious consequences to the U.S. economy and the film industry—the Fox even closed for six months in 1932–33 as a cost-saving measure. In the long run, though, movies proved to be a popular public diversion during the Depression and World War II years.

By the early 1950s, the Fox was finding it difficult to fill all those seats on a regular basis. After many years of declining ticket sales, the owners could no longer sustain the operating losses and wanted to sell the building, but there were no buyers in sight. Midnight organ concerts on Saturday nights were introduced in 1960 to bolster revenues, but the crowds still did not return. Ultimately, San Francisco voters were given a choice—Proposition I (the letter "I"), entitled "Fox Theatre Acquisition," on the November 1961 ballot would have authorized a $1.1 million bond issue for the City to acquire the

Opening night and closing night programs for the Fox Theatre, 1929 and 1963. *Jack Tillmany collection.*

Fox as a performing arts center. Although it needed only a simple majority of the votes cast (50 percent plus one vote), sadly, the measure was defeated with nearly 60 percent "no" votes and barely 40 percent "yes" votes. The Fox was doomed, and the bulldozers arrived just over one year later to demolish the palatial movie palace in order to make way for a high-rise that contains apartments on the upper floors, offices on the lower floors and ground floor retail in a complex that still uses the Fox name. Since the time of the Fox demolition, many other downtown theatres have been demolished or converted to other uses.

Embassy: Under construction at 1125 Market Street in 1906, this theatre opened in 1907 and went through a number of name changes until it reopened as the Embassy in 1927. Although it was one of San Francisco's early "talkie" theatres, it later suffered a decline along with its Market Street neighbors through the years of BART/MUNI construction in the 1960s/1970s. It finally fell victim to the 1989 Loma Prieta earthquake, after which it was closed and demolished.

Esquire: One of downtown's first large theatres, this theatre at 934 Market opened in 1909 and went through several name changes until it became the Esquire in 1940. For the next twenty-five years, it offered first-run films from Universal Studios, ranging from Abbott and Costello comedies to popular horror films. By the mid-1960s, bookings became somewhat seedier, and the theatre was closed and demolished in 1972 to make way for Hallidie Plaza and BART/MUNI's Powell Street station.

Gateway: Opened in 1967 as part of the Golden Gateway complex, this small-screen theatre offered revivals of Hollywood hits, including an annual screening of MGM's 1936 classic *San Francisco*, with Clark Gable, Jeanette MacDonald and Spencer Tracy. Since the 1980s, the site has been operated as a small performing arts center featuring live stage productions.

Golden Gate: This location at Market, Golden Gate and Taylor Streets opened in 1922 and seated 2,844 patrons for both silent films and live vaudeville performances, with sound added in the late 1920s. Twinned in the 1960s, it was closed a decade later and has since been revitalized for live performances.

Orpheum: Opened as the Pantages at 1182 Market Street in 1926, it was renamed Orpheum in 1929—the same year the nearby Fox opened. In 1953, the screen was converted to show "Cinerama" features, which were made using three separate cameras and shown on three projectors running simultaneously. For the next ten years, this was home to long-running engagements including *How the West Was Won*, which ran for more than a

After World War II, the 4,650 seats in the Fox Theatre became increasingly difficult to fill on a regular basis. *OpenSFHistory.*

full year until it closed in December 1963. The Orpheum continued to show movies for a few more years, though the site was long ago converted to a venue for live performances.

Paramount: Built at 1066 Market in 1921 as Granada (before that name was acquired for a new theatre on Mission Street in the Outer Mission/ Excelsior neighborhood), this location with more than 2,600 seats was renamed Paramount in 1931. It hosted the animated Technicolor hit *Gulliver's Travels* in 1939. Often filled to capacity for nighttime performances during World War II, the theatre closed in 1965 and was promptly demolished and replaced by a two-story building that housed a string of small offices/ eateries; in 2019, a new high-rise housing complex was under construction at the Paramount's former location.

Powell: The Powell, built in 1911, was a small (350-seat) second-run house near the cable car turntable. By the 1960s, it was screening revivals of classic films, though it transitioned to showing porn in its final few years. By 1977, it had been closed and replaced with a fast-food outlet.

St. Francis: The St. Francis opened in 1909 at 965 Market Street as the Empress, a vaudeville house with more than 1,400 seats. It was renamed St. Francis in 1925 and converted to show movies. It acquired an art deco marquee in the late 1930s, and in the 1960s, it was twinned/updated with a plain front (with the upstairs renamed Baronet—later, the house became St. Francis I and II). Early in the new millennium, it was still showing mainstream movies—the last movie theatre on Market Street to do so. The place closed with little notice, remained vacant for more than a decade and was demolished in 2013. The site, now combined with the former Kress location, is home to a glass-walled office/retail complex.

State: Built in 1917 at the southeast corner of 4th and Market as the California, this was one of downtown's first movie palaces. Later renamed State, it struggled because most newer downtown theatres were being built several blocks to the west. It closed in 1954 and was demolished in 1961. A decade later, the Roos-Atkins clothing chain built a new store on the site, but that has long since been converted to office space with ground-floor retail.

Strand: The Strand, at 1127 Market Street, catered to bargain-conscious filmgoers with third-run features for much of its history. After suffering more than its neighbors from the decline of the mid–Market Street neighborhood (even after BART/MUNI construction was completed), it began screening adult videos. Closed after a 2003 police raid, it never reopened and is now a live performance site/café operated by A.C.T. (American Conservatory Theater).

Telenews: Located near the Esquire and the Warfield, Telenews opened at 930 Market in 1939 with film coverage of the Nazi invasion of Poland. It operated a newsreel/travelogue format until 1967, when it was closed and demolished to make way for Hallidie Plaza and the Powell Street BART/MUNI station.

United Artists: Opened at 1077 Market in 1912, this location went through several name changes until 1931, when it became United Artists. For many years, it was home to long-running engagements of blockbuster films, including *West Side Story* (forty-six weeks in 1962), *Lawrence of Arabia* (forty-seven weeks in 1963) and *Sound of Music* (ninety-two weeks in 1965–66). In 1972, it was renamed Market Street Cinema and became home to adult films and, later, explicit live performances. It was closed in 2013 and demolished in 2016.

Warfield: Opened at 982 Market in 1922, just after the nearby Golden Gate, the Warfield was another large theatre with more than 2,600 seats.

This location was still enjoying long lines of nighttime customers well into the 1950s for films such as *Show Boat* (in 1951) and the wide-screen rerelease of *Gone With the Wind* (in 1954). Closed as a movie theatre in the 1970s, it continues as a live performance/concert venue.

The Mission District had a large number of movie houses for decades, some of which rivaled downtown theatres in terms of sheer opulence. Sadly, those that remain today are often shadows of their former selves, though there are signs of revitalization taking place at several of them.

El Capitan: The once-grand facade remains, but the marquee is no longer lighted, and the auditorium was gutted more than sixty years ago to make way for an open-air parking lot.

Grand: Opened in 1940 as a single-level movie theatre, the building was a retail outlet for several decades. Now restored, the building is available for rent as an event venue known as Gray Area, though the classic Grand marquee remains.

New Mission: Among the most prominent of Mission Street's row of theatres, the New Mission opened in 1916. It was designed by the local Reid Brothers firm and was converted to sound and extensively remodeled in art deco style by architect Timothy Pflueger in the early 1930s. It remains best known for its tall vertical sign—a Mission Street landmark for more than seventy-five years. The theatre closed in 1993 and went through a sad decline as a discount furniture outlet. Named a local landmark in 2004, the building was thoroughly restored and opened in 2015 as a multiplex cinema/dining/beverages location, with its grand marquee shining brightly once again.

Roosevelt/York: The restored theatre on 24th Street is now a performance venue for women in the arts.

Roxie: Operating under various names since 1909, the Roxie (since 1933) states that it is the oldest continuously operating theatre in the United States. After making a comeback in 1976 after a decade of screening pornographic films, the Roxie has since featured art-house and independent films.

Victoria: This one-time vaudeville house, which dates back to 1908, has been revamped into a venue for stage plays, live concerts, musicals and film festivals.

Some large neighborhood theatres that have also transitioned include:

Alhambra: A lavish Polk Street theatre when it opened in 1926, the Alhambra suffered from a lack of available nearby parking in later years of the twentieth century. It closed in 1998 and was replaced with a health club, though most of the building's architecture was saved.

Avenue: Built in 1927 as a neighborhood anchor on San Bruno Avenue in the Portola, the Avenue experienced the same decline in attendance that impacted theatres nationwide and closed in 1984. After the theatre sat vacant for more than thirty years, new owners partnered with neighbors and a local merchant group to secure grant money and donations to restore the massive vertical neon sign. Commitments have been made for some of the ground-floor retail space, and efforts are underway to secure a tenant for the large auditorium.

Granada: A popular neighborhood house in the Excelsior district, this location closed in 1982 and has recently served as a Goodwill Industries retail outlet.

Haight: Closed as a film theatre in 1964, it was a Haight-Ashbury event venue for another decade before closing again and being demolished in 1979.

Harding: Built in 1926 on Divisadero Street, the theatre continued showing films and was also used by The Lamplighters live theatrical group during the 1960s. It was the site of a Grateful Dead concert in 1971 and then used as a church until 2004. It then sat vacant until being reopened as a bar/gaming arcade/music venue in 2017.

Noe: A staple of Noe Valley for only fifteen years, this was among the last theatres built in San Francisco before World War II and the first to be demolished after the war (in 1952).

Northpoint: Opened in 1967, the Northpoint was home to such long-running hits as *2001: A Space Odyssey*, *Midnight Cowboy* and *The Exorcist*. It closed in 1997, and the building is now occupied by offices and a Goodwill Industries retail store.

Royal: This 1,500-seat house was built in 1916 on Polk Street. Closed in 1998, it was demolished in 2003 and replaced with housing and ground-floor retail; the exterior architectural elements were preserved.

The sprawling western neighborhoods of the Richmond and Sunset Districts were also home to many now-closed screens:

Alexandria: Built with Egyptian-style architecture in 1923, it was remodeled in Moderne style in 1941, converted to a triplex in 1976 and closed in 2004. The site is set to reopen as a swimming complex, with new housing already completed on the 18th Avenue parking lot site.

Bridge: Opened in 1939 with second-runs, by the 1950s, this became a venue for international films, often with extended engagements, such as *Zorba the Greek* (twenty-nine weeks in 1965) and *Georgy Girl* (twenty-three weeks in 1966–67). The location closed in December 2012 and is now a baseball academy with the classic sign preserved.

Coliseum: Opened in 1918, the theatre converted to sound in 1929 but was damaged by the 1989 Loma Prieta earthquake and never reopened. The building was converted to housing with ground-floor retail.

Coronet: Opened in 1949, the Coronet closed in 2005 and was demolished in 2007 and replaced with a senior housing complex. The Coronet hosted many long-running hits: *Around the World in 80 Days* (all-time San Francisco record—ninety-six weeks in 1956–58), *Ben Hur* (seventy-five weeks in 1959–

Coronet Theatre, located at 3575 Geary near Arguello Boulevard, at the time of its final closing in March 2005. Demolition began in 2007, and the site is now home to a senior housing complex. *Western Neighborhoods Project.*

61), *Funny Girl* (fifty-nine weeks in 1968–69), *My Fair Lady* (fifty weeks in 1964–65), *Oklahoma!* (forty-four weeks in 1956), *Hawaii* (thirty-five weeks in 1966–67), *Camelot* (thirty-five weeks in 1967–68), *The Godfather* (thirty-two weeks in 1972) and *Star Wars* (twenty-nine weeks in 1977).

El Rey: Opened in 1931, the El Rey closed in 1977 and was home to a church from 1977 to 2015, then purchased by a group of investors. The building (also home to the first Gap retail store in 1967) was granted landmark status by City Hall in 2017; several possible future uses are now under consideration.

Irving: Opened in 1926, this was demolished and replaced with an apartment building in 1962.

Parkside: Opened in 1928, this was renamed Fox Parkside in 1965 and lost its iconic red marquee. The space was reconfigured in 1976 and closed in 1988; it is now home to small businesses, with condos on the upper floors.

Surf: Opened in 1926 as Parkview, this was renamed Sunset in 1937 and then Surf in 1957, when it began showing classic films; it closed in 1985. The building has been home to a church for many years.

The Balboa Theatre, opened in 1926 and twinned in 1978, remains an anchor in the Outer Richmond district—one of a handful of neighborhood screens that is still open and thriving in the twenty-first century. *Original artwork by Robin Galante (used with permission).*

Within the western neighborhoods, theatres still in operation include the Balboa, 4-Star, UA Twin Cinemas-Stonestown, and CineArts at the Empire. In 2019, plans were underway for a twelve-screen complex to be constructed atop shops and restaurants at the old Macy's/Emporium Stonestown property, thus calling into question what will become of the vintage 1970 UA-Twin Cinemas on the western portion of the property.

Finally, the drive-ins that offered exciting entertainment that local kids of today will never experience:

Geneva: Opened in 1950 on Carter Street just off Geneva Avenue in Daly City, near the Cow Palace. The site operated as a single-screen for more than twenty-five years, and additional screens were added in the 1970s. It closed in 2000 and was demolished in 2002. The nearness of the Cow Palace often produced monumental traffic jams when events at the two locations ended at the same time.

Mission: Located just over the border in San Mateo County, the Mission Drive-In advertised a San Francisco address of 5500 Mission Street. It opened on Guttenburg Street in a hilly part of Daly City in 1951 and closed in 1976. Both the Geneva and Mission drive-ins had well-deserved reputations as hotspots for rough clientele—public intoxication, fistfights and even gunfire were regular occurrences in later years.

Terrace: Technically, the only drive-in located within San Francisco city limits was the short-lived Terrace on Alemany Boulevard near the Alemany Farmers' Market. Long plagued by foggy nights, the location only operated from 1951 to 1954, and the site is now part of the Interstate 280 right-of-way.

In the end, though, theatres may be on the verge of a comeback—as evidenced by the refurbishment/reopening of the New Mission Theatre and restoration of the Avenue Theatre marquee on San Bruno Avenue. Likewise, the long-closed Presidio Theatre, built in 1939 by the WPA on the one-time military base, is scheduled for a 2019 reopening.

At the same time, livestreaming and video services such as Netflix have challenged the viability of brick-and-mortar theatres in much the same way that television impacted them over sixty years ago.

Several newer screens along Van Ness Avenue have gone dark, including the Regency I and II at Van Ness Avenue and Sutter Street, which were closed in 1998 and 2000, respectively, plus the nearby four-screen glass-box Galaxy, built in 1984, which ceased operations in 2005 and was demolished in 2011 for an apartment tower. More recently, the AMC–Van Ness, a fourteen-screen multiplex opened in a former Cadillac showroom at Van Ness Avenue and O'Farrell Street in 1998, was abruptly shut down in February 2019. Meanwhile, the Opera Plaza four-screen cinema at Van Ness and Golden Gate Avenues, in operation since 1984, has been the focus of possible new uses by the property owner since at least 2017.

Dwarfed by numerous larger structures, the 1898 Ferry Building, now home to an artisanal market hall, still welcomes visitors who arrive on a revitalized ferry fleet. Buildings in the area date from pre-1900 to 2018. *Meric Dagly photo.*

3
Repurposed Places

As San Francisco continues to change, many businesses and institutions have disappeared from the local landscape. Those that remain often hold cherished memories from the past and can be quickly spotted and identified by longtime residents.

In addition, many structures such as banks, offices, hospitals, movie theatres, houses of worship and others have been repurposed for new uses. Rather than being torn down like so many of their predecessors (Fox Theatre, Montgomery Block, City of Paris and thousands of Victorian homes), a lot of older buildings have been saved by designers who adapt them to new uses, thus preserving important structural features that continue to be part of the local architectural mosaic.

Here's a brief look at many splendid survivors—some of them changed a bit, others still true to their original purpose and plenty now totally reimagined.

BANKS

The arrival of ATMs in the 1980s, plus direct deposit of paychecks and other recurring payments, online banking and merger activity in the financial services industry are all factors that have contributed to fewer bank buildings.

Here are some adaptations of well-known locations:

Bank of America/1 Powell Street: Opened in 1921 as the new Bank of Italy headquarters (renamed Bank of America in 1929) and later home to a variety of administrative offices, including the Women's Banking Department on the second floor (from 1921 to 1946) and a once-large but now defunct Travelers Cheques operation, it was converted early in the 2000s to apartments on the upper floors with ground-floor retail.

Bank of America/1 South Van Ness Avenue: Built in the late 1950s as the bank's credit card and data center (along with other administrative departments) with a large branch on the ground floor and a significant indoor parking facility, the building was sold early in the twenty-first century and is now occupied by numerous City and County of San Francisco government agency offices.

Bank of America/400 Castro Street: Originally built as a Bank of Italy branch in 1922, the building housed banking operations until Hibernia Bank was acquired in the late 1980s, when this branch was relocated to Hibernia's former building one block away at 18th and Castro. This site was then home to a variety of different retail stores over the years.

Bank of America/550 Montgomery Street: Built as Bank of Italy headquarters in 1908, it continued to house bank offices on upper floors and a ground-floor branch after the headquarters was moved to Powell Street in 1921. Bank of America recently sold the building, and the upper floors are now rented to various office tenants and a private club, while the ground floor is leased to a luxury men's retail store, with tailoring and a barbershop in the building's old basement vault area.

Hibernia Bank: The ornate banking temple at 1 Jones Street was constructed in 1892 and survived the earthquake and fire of 1906 reasonably intact. It was one of the last of the old-time banking temples, complete with marble floors, a stained-glass skylight and enormous vaults, and was run by the Tobin Brothers, who only reluctantly agreed to open branches in the 1950s but staunchly refused to issue credit cards. For decades, the bank had a loyal, multiethnic clientele based on their favorable interest rates on savings and loans. In the 1980s, however, Hibernia was acquired by Bank of America, and the iconic old main office was closed. After serving as home to the Tenderloin Police Station for a few years, the building was boarded up, covered with graffiti and became a haven for those involved in drugs and alcohol. The site was eventually purchased by a group of investors, and a massive $15 million restoration was completed,

Where the cable car turns — No. 1 Powell Street, San Francisco — Day and Night Branch of Bank of America

Number ONE...the bank that knows California

With resources of more than nine billion dollars, Bank of America is the world's largest bank. It is owned by more than 200,000 stockholders.

★ ★ ★

When you travel always carry Bank of America Travelers Cheques

A famous address — 1 Powell Street, San Francisco — for years the Day and Night Branch of Bank of America — the world's *number one* bank.

Throughout California you will find this bank — 580 branches in 350 communities — meeting every local banking need. This unique

statewide bank serves the out-of-state businessman by providing him with industrial information... sales and market data...collection and credit information.

All reasons why you should make this bank *your* number one choice in the West. Your letter will receive our prompt attention.

Bank of America
NATIONAL TRUST AND SAVINGS ASSOCIATION
MEMBER FEDERAL DEPOSIT INSURANCE CORPORATION

HEAD OFFICES: SAN FRANCISCO, LOS ANGELES

Magazine ad for Bank of America "Travelers Cheques" showing 1 Powell Street building in 1956. Today, the structure has been converted to apartments on the upper floors, with retail space on the ground floor. Travelers cheques are no longer being marketed. *Author's collection.*

with the marble floors, skylight and vaults restored; the building is now available for rent as an event venue.

Federal Reserve Bank: The imposing granite building at 400 Sansome Street was built in classic Beaux-Arts style in the 1920s, with a more modern yet classic upper section added later. When the Federal Reserve moved to larger facilities at 101 Market Street in 1983, the Sansome Street location was sold to private developers. A large law firm occupied the space until 2002, and today, there are multiple office tenants on the upper floors, while the main banking hall is regularly rented out as an upscale event venue.

Savings Union Bank: Constructed in 1910 as part of the grand post-fire rebuilding of the downtown area, the structure at 1 Grant Avenue was designed as one of the great banking temples of the era. During a period of mergers among financial services firms, it acquired several different names. By the 1990s, the structure was home to a clothing retailer, and in 2017, it reemerged as the Ice Cream Museum.

GOVERNMENT/MILITARY

Government facilities once dotted the San Francisco Bay Area landscape. From 1988 through the mid-1990s, the federal government closed or repurposed numerous Northern California locations for private use—Hamilton Air Force Base (Marin County), Mather Air Force Base (Sacramento County), Alameda Naval Air Station (Alameda County), Fort Ord (Monterey County), Moffett Field Naval Air Station (Santa Clara County), Presidio of Monterey (Monterey County), Sacramento Army Depot (Sacramento County), Mare Island Naval Shipyard (Solano County), Oakland Naval Supply Center (Alameda County), Oakland Army Hospital (Alameda County), McClellan Air Force Base (Sacramento County) and Oakland Army Base (Alameda County).

Within San Francisco, there were also several major closures of government-owned facilities, including the following:

Fort Mason: The area came into use as a military fortification during the Civil War and remained a vital part of coastal defenses for more than one hundred years. Particularly during World War II, Fort Mason was the headquarters of the San Francisco Point of Embarkation for well over 1.5 million troops headed for destinations in the Pacific. By the mid-1960s, army use had declined, and the site fell under the control of the National Park Service following the creation of the Golden Gate National Recreation Area in 1972. Today, numerous nonprofit organizations, such as art and music galleries, restaurants, bookstores, museums and other groups promoting arts and culture, occupy many of the historic structures.

Old U.S. Mint: The Old Mint at 5th and Mission Streets, constructed in 1869, was one of the few downtown buildings to survive the earthquake and fire of 1906. The superintendent successfully persuaded troops to spare the structure when many nearby buildings were being dynamited in a futile effort to stop the fires. Largely unused until recently, the Old Mint is now in a gradual process of restoration and a venue for regular history activities and presentations.

Presidio of San Francisco: A coastal location fortified by the Spanish government in 1776, the site passed to Mexico after its War

Old U.S. Mint at 5th and Mission Streets, circa 2005. The old building was saved even after operations moved to a new site on Duboce Avenue in 1937. *Alvis Hendley photo/Noe Hill collection.*

Original interior light fixtures at the Old U.S. Mint. *Judy Hitzeman photo.*

of Independence with Spain and was eventually ceded to the U.S. government in 1848. It long served as an outpost of the U.S. Army at the entrance to San Francisco Bay. As part of a 1989 Base Realignment and Closure Act, Congress voted to end the Presidio's role as an active U.S. military base, and in October 1994, the property passed into the hands of the National Park Service.

In 1996, Congress created the Presidio Trust to manage the interior portions of the property, with the National Park Service managing the coastal perimeter. The Presidio Trust achieved its goal of financial self-sufficiency by 2005 and is now home to a number of operations, including restored housing, the Walt Disney Family Museum, the Bay School (a private elementary school), Letterman Digital Arts Center (operated by Lucasfilm), open space habitats at Crissy Field and various low-key retail and food service outlets. Many of the historic structures, along with the Presidio of San Francisco National Cemetery, have been preserved.

Hospitals

Changes in health care practices, including a greater emphasis on outpatient services and much shorter stays for many inpatient procedures, plus multiple acquisitions and mergers, have all contributed to changes in hospital facilities. Many solid old buildings have been repurposed for a variety of new uses.

French Hospital: The buildings on Geary Boulevard near 5th Avenue were acquired by Kaiser Permanente when that organization took over French Hospital in 1989. Many structures remain in use, but the former four-story redbrick nurses' residence at the northeast corner of 6th Avenue and Anza Street has been leased to the University of San Francisco, located one mile away, for student housing since 2000.

Notre Dame Hospital: The multibuilding complex at Van Ness Avenue and Broadway was originally built as Dante Sanitarium in 1909 and later became Notre Dame Hospital, run by the Sisters of Mercy. The location was converted to senior housing in the 1970s, with extensive upgrades completed in the twenty-first century, and is now a low-income senior housing complex for 250 residents.

Shriner's Hospital: The redbrick structure along 19th Avenue has been a familiar sight to motorists since the early 1920s. The facility was expanded around 1970, but by the 1990s, the decision was made to relocate to the Sacramento area. With its original building achieving landmark status, developers rehabbed the main portion into offices and community areas for a new senior housing complex built on the western portion of the property at 20th Avenue and Lawton Street. New, individually owned townhomes were added to the southern part of the property from 19th Avenue to 20th Avenue.

Southern Pacific Hospital: Built in 1908 to replace a previous company-owned facility destroyed in 1906, this hospital served the needs of railroad employees and their families, as well as the company's many retirees. As railroad employment declined, and after the introduction of Medicare for seniors in 1966, fewer patients were treated here, and many opted to seek care in other facilities. The hospital was sold in 1968 but never regained viability, and it finally closed in 1974. After extensive remodeling, it reopened in 1981 as Mercy Terrace, a senior housing facility.

St. Joseph's Hospital: Built in classic Beaux-Arts style in 1928 on Buena Vista Avenue, and with magnificent views of San Francisco, the building operated as a full-service hospital for more than fifty years.

Old St. Joseph's Hospital on Buena Vista Avenue was converted to condominiums in the 1980s. *Alvis Hendley photo/Noe Hill Collection.*

In 1979, it was closed and converted to individually owned Park Hill condominiums that opened in the 1980s. Units now sell for well over $1,000 per square foot.

U.S. Public Health Service Hospital: The U.S. Marine Hospital was built on a site in the Presidio. Overlooking the Richmond District, it evolved into the U.S. Public Health Service Hospital by 1932 and was used as a research facility and for serving local community needs. When the hospital closed in 1981, the building was used as classroom space by federal government agencies. In 2010, after demolition of certain portions of the complex, the vintage 1932 structure was reopened as an apartment building.

HOUSES OF WORSHIP

Membership and attendance have declined at many houses of worship over the past few decades, forcing many older congregations to confront serious cost issues related to ongoing operations and deferred building maintenance—though this situation is far from being new.

Within the Archdiocese of San Francisco, there was an official 2017 merger of St. Monica and St. Thomas the Apostle parishes in the Richmond District, with both churches and schools remaining open but under a single parish organization. Nearly fifty-five years earlier, in 1963, there was a merger of an older Jewish congregation, Temple Beth Israel on Geary near Fillmore, with the newer Temple Judea on Brotherhood Way. Ten years prior to that, Temple United Methodist Church was built on Junipero Serra Boulevard near 19th Avenue as a combination of four older downtown congregations. Such changes continue today.

Congregation B'nai David: Built to replace a prior temple lost in 1906, this temple serving a small Orthodox Jewish community was located on 19th Street in the Mission District. Membership began to decline by the time of World War II, and the congregation shuttered the building by the 1970s. Acquired by a private developer, the site was converted for use as apartments in 1981, with its stucco facade and exterior architectural details preserved.

Fourth Church of Christ, Scientist: Constructed in 1923 at Funston Avenue and Clement Street in the Richmond District, the classic Greek Revival building with soaring columns facing Park Presidio Drive served the congregation until 2009. A decline in membership and the high cost of building maintenance led the group to sell the building to the Internet Archive, which has preserved the exterior.

Golden Gate Lutheran Church: Located at 601 Dolores Street, the redbrick structure was built in 1910 facing Dolores Park. When the congregation disbanded, the 20,000-plus-square-foot property was converted to a large home with twelve-plus rooms. Listed for sale again in 2011, the building was purchased and has been in use since 2015 as an expanded space for the middle school campus of the nearby Children's Day School.

Greater Gethsemane Church: Originally built in 1909 as St. Paul's German Methodist Church on Page Street near Octavia Street in Hayes Valley, the craftsman-style building has been on the market for just under $3 million for several years. It is located on a block with zoning generally limited to residential, and it also has historical designation, limiting the scope of any architectural changes.

Macang Monastery: In 1899, Holy Cross Church opened at Divisadero and Eddy Streets in the Western Addition neighborhood. Damaged in 1906, it was quickly restored. By 1989, the twin-towered stone building was suffering from both Loma Prieta earthquake damage and declining membership. The property was sold to developers, who eventually converted part of the church into condominiums and the main sanctuary into a new Buddhist temple, including an adjacent building long used as a parish hall. That structure was once the original wooden St. Patrick's Church built on Market Street in 1854 at the site of today's Palace Hotel. It was moved to Eddy Street between Octavia and Laguna in 1872, where it served for nearly twenty years as the now-defunct St. John the Baptist Church (the members of which were merged into the then-new St. Mary's Cathedral on nearby Van Ness Avenue in 1891). The old building was then moved seven blocks west to serve as the original Holy Cross Church for nearly a decade before becoming a parish hall in 1899. That small wooden building with the construction materials that came around the Horn by ship is the second-oldest religious building (after Mission Dolores) in San Francisco and the only one that has occupied three different locations while serving four different congregations.

Sacred Heart Church: Completed in 1898 at Fillmore and Fell Streets, the imposing church on a hill—with a bell tower visible even from the downtown area—suffered from a serious decline in attendance beginning in the 1960s, as well as deferred maintenance. The 1989 Loma Prieta earthquake damaged the ceiling so severely that heavy-duty netting had to be installed to protect visitors from falling plaster. There were significant efforts to preserve the building, but it was eventually sold and now houses a roller-skating rink.

Second Church of Christ, Scientist: Built in 1905, the massive domed structure on Dolores Park near Cumberland Street is a neighborhood icon that had a large number of active members for more than a century. In this millennium, though, the congregation was facing the prospects of declining membership and increased maintenance costs. Ultimately, the decision was made to relocate the congregation to a new site in the Mission District and sell the Dolores Street property for development in 2012. By 2016, the interior had been extensively remodeled and creatively repurposed into a series of four architecturally unique private residences while preserving the building's exterior.

St. Brigid's Church: The imposing Romanesque stone structure has been anchoring the southwest corner of Van Ness Avenue and Broadway since 1902 and survived both the 1906 and the 1989 earthquakes. In a highly controversial decision, the San Francisco Archdiocese closed the building in 1994. Amid a hotly contested debate, the building was sold to the privately run Academy of Art College in 2005. The art school continues to operate there and has preserved the building in accordance with its local landmark

into a separate structure once again, with upper-floor office space and ground-floor retail tenants.

Liberty House: Opened in 1974 on the southern portion of the old City of Paris site, Liberty House displayed a tan travertine exterior with windows only on the ground floor and top-floor offices. After being acquired by Macy's for its men's building in 1984, the structure was sold in 2016. As of mid-2019, an extensive interior and exterior remodel is underway, with a planned mix of ground-floor retail spaces and upper-floor offices in a glass-walled structure.

Masonic Temple: Built at Van Ness Avenue and Oak Street just after the 1906 disaster, the building was home to Masonic Lodge activities until 1978, when a decline in membership prompted its sale. Beginning in 1984, a gradual rehab process has now turned the structure into an office building that is home to several City and county government departments, including the Rent Board, Arts Commission, Project Homeless Connect, Veterans Service and Department of Public Health offices.

Mothers Building at the Zoo: Dedicated to Delia Fleishhacker by her sons Herbert and Mortimer, who were early and longtime benefactors of the San Francisco Zoo, the building was constructed in 1925 as a place of rest for mothers and their children. In 1938, murals by Dorothy Puccinelli and Helen Forbes were added to the upper interior walls through a federal grant as part of the WPA. Sadly, the building was the victim of deferred maintenance, and the murals sustained significant water damage over the years. Thankfully, a major restoration project is underway so that the building, closed to the public since 2002, may soon reopen as a visitor center.

Old *Chronicle* Building: Located at Market, Geary and Kearny Streets, the reddish masonry structure was home to the newspaper from 1890 until

Part of a four-panel mural, *Noah and His Ark—The Waters Subsiding and Renewal* was painted in 1938 by WPA artists Dorothy Puccinelli and Helen Forbes. *Richard Rothman photo.*

1924, when it made the move to Fifth and Mission Streets. Continuing its life as a standard office building, it was "modernized" in 1962 with the installation of aluminum paneling. By 2004, new owners received approval to restore the original facade, convert the building to residential use and construct an addition adjacent to the existing structure. Since late 2007, the building has been operating as the Ritz-Carlton Club and Residences.

Penney's Department Store: Located at 5th and Market Streets, this 1909 building was long occupied by retailer J.C. Penney (and earlier, Hale Brothers), though it sat idle for several years after Penney's departed San Francisco in early 1971. It was carefully renovated and converted to office space on the upper floors, with ground-floor retail tenants by the early 1990s.

San Francisco Armory: Built in 1914 for the National Guard, the Moorish-inspired castle-like building at 14th and Mission Streets has had an eclectic lineup of tenants in its one-hundred-plus years. In addition to its original use, it also served as a sports venue in the 1920s and was the location for prize fights, then was used by the military during World War II. It was largely unused after 1946, and by the mid-1970s, it saw occasional use by some Hollywood studios and the San Francisco Opera as a construction facility for stage sets. In early 2007, an announcement was made that the building had been sold to a pornographic film production company, which used the site for the next ten years. In January 2018, the building was sold to an investment firm that plans to convert the top two floors to office space and lease the rest of the building to manufacturing companies.

4

Splendid Survivors

Many cherished San Francisco landmarks have come and gone over the years, yet we are grateful for those that have survived long periods of time relatively unscathed. In many cases, they have become integral parts of the local landscape reminding us of the way things used to be.

In trying to build on this natural phenomenon in 2013, a local history group, San Francisco Heritage, created an online guide to celebrate iconic eating and drinking establishments that were contributing to the culture, character and lore of San Francisco. The list was an instant hit, and it spawned additional interest in historic preservation.

Two years later, local government expanded the concept by creating the San Francisco Legacy Business Registry. The registry is open to businesses that have been in existence for thirty years or longer, have been nominated by a member of the Board of Supervisors or mayor and can prove that they have made a significant impact on the history or culture of their neighborhood in a hearing before the Small Business Commission. Only three hundred businesses can be nominated per year, and all applicants must agree to maintain the historical name and essential business operations, physical features, craft and traditions of their businesses. Once a business is registered, there are certain financial incentives for ongoing compliance with the guidelines.

Legacy Businesses are longstanding community-serving companies that are recognized as valuable cultural assets to San Francisco. Helping to preserve such businesses is believed to be critical to keeping San Francisco a unique and special place. Legacy Businesses range in industry, size, tradition, history, products and services and include restaurants, retail stores, bars, service providers, manufacturers, artists and more. Initially, many of these businesses were located in older neighborhoods, including Downtown, Chinatown, North Beach and the Mission. Today, there are more than two hundred participating businesses in virtually every neighborhood.

In addition to such new initiatives, many San Francisco buildings have miraculously continued to retain their classic appearances, as well as their original daily uses, for well over a century. Here are just a few of them.

Bank of California: Constructed in 1908, the classic banking temple at 400 California Street replaced one that was lost in the 1906 earthquake and fire. The site was acquired by Union Bank in 1996, and in 2008, Bank of Tokyo-Mitsubishi acquired control of the business that now operates under the slightly revised name UnionBank.

Civic Infrastructure: San Francisco residents of today owe a significant debt of gratitude to their predecessors, who taxed themselves heavily to rebuild after the earthquake and fire of 1906. From the classic Beaux-Arts Civic Center to an extensive system of public transit, schools, water and a high-pressure fire

The gigantic Twin Peaks Reservoir, divided into two separate sections (in case of a failure in one section) was dedicated in 1912 with a public open house in the then-dry portion. Maintained and strengthened over the years, it remains a vital—though largely underappreciated—component of the City's infrastructure. *OpenSFHistory.*

suppression system, plus many new public educational facilities, much of what is enjoyed today came about in the aftermath of disaster.

Cliff House: There have been three different Cliff House buildings since the mid-1800s with multiple different exterior finishes. As part of the Golden Gate National Recreation Area since 1972, the present building underwent a significant renovation by the National Park Service in 2005 that removed the post–World War II exterior and restored its 1909 appearance.

This 1970s version of the current Cliff House building, with hand-painted blue waves around the roofline, replaced the dark wood and neon lettering from the post–World War II model. It was a popular destination for local college students during its weekly ten-cent beer night. *Author's collection.*

Today's Cliff House viewed from Ocean Beach. *Wikimedia Commons.*

Street-corner flower vendors have been beloved fixtures on downtown streets for over one hundred years. Though fewer of them exist today, they continue to provide a touch of enjoyment throughout the year. *Glenn D. Koch collection.*

Downtown Flower Stands: For more than one hundred years, many independently owned flower vendors have brightened the local scene with their stands.

Emporium: A mainstay of the mid–Market Street area since the late 1800s, the building's classic facade survived the 1906 earthquake and fire, though the store itself had to be gutted and rebuilt. Nearly one hundred years later, when the property was taken over as part of a new Bloomingdale's store, the building's classic front wall and dome were preserved and included in an expansion of the adjacent San Francisco Shopping Center.

Lowell High School: Built as Lowell High School in 1911, the redbrick structure at Hayes Street and Masonic Avenue was replaced by a new campus on Eucalyptus Drive near Lake Merced in 1962. Today, the school's old home is operated as the John Adams campus of City College of San Francisco. Lowell's class of 1962, the last to graduate before the move, celebrated its fifty-year reunion in the old building.

Old St. Mary's: When it was dedicated on Christmas Eve 1854, the redbrick structure was the tallest building in California. Old St. Mary's was designated an official San Francisco Landmark when that program began in April 1968.

Old St. Mary's was built as San Francisco's first Roman Catholic cathedral in 1854. The adjacent office building on California Street was constructed 110 years later. *OpenSFHistory.*

Pacific Telephone & Telegraph: Located at 140 New Montgomery Street, this was the tallest building in San Francisco from 1925 to 1964 (tied with the Russ Building, which opened in 1927). Once planned as a condominium conversion, the financial recession of 2007–09 scuttled those plans. After a $100 million restoration in 2012, Yelp acquired space for its headquarters, signing a lease as the building's primary tenant, thus preserving the site as a major downtown office building.

Palace Hotel: The original Palace Hotel opened in 1875, and upon completion, it was the largest and grandest hotel in California, as well as San Francisco's tallest building (for a decade). In spite of certain fire-suppression systems built into the hotel's design, it suffered a fire in 1906 and had to be demolished. The replacement structure on the same site opened to great acclaim in 1909. In 1923, President Harding died in the Presidential Suite. In 1954, the hotel was acquired by the Sheraton chain and displayed the hyphenated name Sheraton-Palace for the next four decades until after a 1989–91 restoration, when it again became simply the Palace.

The Palace Hotel's Garden Court (also known as the Palm Court) remains a classic dining space, evoking memories of the original 1875 building. *Dllu Photography, Wikimedia Commons.*

MODERN NEW STORE
at Geary Blvd. and Masonic
...to be opened soon

Applications
FOR EMPLOYMENT
Now Being Accepted

Many interesting and well paid positions are now available in selling and non-selling at Sears' new Geary Store
to be opened in the near future.

Apply...
PERSONNEL OFFICE
3rd FLOOR, PARKING
LOT ENTRANCE
Geary at Masonic
San Francisco

You'll enjoy working for Sears, Roebuck and Co., and
participating in its many employee benefits which include
Profit Sharing, Group Insurance, Hospitalization, Discount
Privileges, Paid Vacations and Holidays.

Applications will be accepted daily 9:30 a.m. until 4:30 p.m.

SEARS, ROEBUCK AND CO., GEARY BLVD. AT MASONIC AVE.

For decades, the Sears store at Geary and Masonic Avenue displayed a green neon sign with a stylized letter "S" that was visible throughout the community. Many people still recall the strong scent of fresh popcorn that permeated the entire building. Sadly, business at this location declined over the years, and when the store closed in 1990, the number of employees had dropped from an initial 1,500 to about 200. Today, the site is known as City Center—home to a complex of smaller retail businesses. *Western Neighborhoods Project.*

Sears, Roebuck: Sears opened its first San Francisco store in the Mission in 1929, and it remained in business until 1975. In 1951, the firm expanded its local presence with a vast new building and attached parking lots at Geary Boulevard and Masonic Avenue on the site of the old Calvary Cemetery.

St. Francis Fountain: San Francisco's oldest ice cream parlor has been serving up treats and light meals since it first opened in 1918 at 24th and York Streets in the Mission District.

St. Ignatius Church: Built in 1914 to replace a structure lost in 1906, the twin towers continue to cast their mark on the City's horizon at Fulton Street and Parker Avenue. In addition to its traditional use by the adjacent University of San Francisco, the church once again became an official parish of the Archdiocese of San Francisco in 1994 after having been stripped of parish status in 1863.

Tadich Grill: Tracing its origins back to the days of the Gold Rush in 1849, Tadich's has been in operation at its current location on California Street since 1967 and is the oldest continuously run restaurant in California.

Temple Sherith Israel: Located at California and Webster Streets since 1905, the classic steel-domed synagogue recently underwent a massive earthquake retrofit program and interior restoration and is home to a thriving congregation that dates back to the Gold Rush, making it one of the oldest synagogues in the United States.

Victorian Homes: In spite of thousands of demolitions over the years, hundreds of these structures located in neighborhoods across San Francisco are still "home" to many individuals and families.

A favorite of San Franciscans and visitors alike—the "Painted Ladies." These well-maintained Victorian homes on the 700 block of Steiner Street opposite Alamo Square in the Western Addition neighborhood were built between 1892 and 1896. *Mike Oria Photography (used with permission).*

5

Visions of Days Gone By

A s we appreciate what remains today, we also remember a few of the lost components of San Francisco's storied past, with some places sorely missed—and some less so.

The Montgomery Block, a four-story office building at the southeast corner of Montgomery and Washington Streets in the Financial District, was built in 1853 as San Francisco's first fireproof and earthquake-resistant building. At the time of construction, it was the tallest building west of the Mississippi River and was home to generations of business offices and artist studios. It was unceremoniously demolished in 1959 to make room for a parking lot—a site which eventually saw the beginning of construction on the Transamerica Pyramid in 1969.

The magnificent 1929 Fox Theatre on Market Street fell to the wrecking ball in 1963.

Sutro Baths, Fleishhacker Pool and Playland were all demolished between 1966 and 1972—losses that became more acutely felt as time passed.

The Embarcadero Freeway, built in 1958, was damaged by the 1989 Loma Prieta earthquake and demolished in 1991—to much public rejoicing.

Some losses occurred because temporary structures were demolished after they had served their intended short-term uses. Many of these memorable buildings were constructed for various fairs, including the Midwinter Fair of 1894 in Golden Gate Park, the 1915 Panama-Pacific International Exposition in the Marina and the 1939–40 Golden Gate International Exposition held on Treasure Island.

SAN FRANCISCO EXAMINER ART SUPPLEMENT
JANUARY 21, 1894.

ELECTRICAL FOUNTAIN AND THE MANUFACTURES AND LIBERAL ARTS BUILDING

Above: Souvenir of Midwinter Fair of 1894 held in Golden Gate Park. *Glenn D. Koch collection.*

Left: The Panama-Pacific International Exposition of 1915 welcomed the world to a city rebuilt after the earthquake and fire of 1906. *Glenn D. Koch collection.*

A World's Fair on an island in the middle of San Francisco Bay delighted visitors for two seasons in 1939–40. The property eventually came under the control of the U.S. Navy until it was finally returned to the City in the late 1990s. Treasure Island is now being redeveloped as a new San Francisco neighborhood. *Author's collection.*

Changing tastes have also impacted the tourism industry. While the modern pink-blue motif and revolving rooftop sign of the Jack Tar Hotel on Van Ness Avenue were heralded upon its opening in 1960, the building was subdued with a cream-color paint job by the 1980s. Business eventually declined, and it was demolished in 2013 for a new state-of-the-art California Pacific Medical Center hospital facility, which opened in March 2019. Another "modern" lodging, the low-rise Del Webb's Towne House, opened in 1960 on the site of the old Crystal Palace Market at 8th and Market Streets, but after a 1980s conversion to apartments, it was eventually demolished and replaced with a high-rise housing complex that will be completed in 2020. Likewise, the venerable 1950s Roberts-at-the-Beach Motel on Sloat Boulevard slid into a level of seediness in the twenty-first century and was demolished for a new five-story condo complex set to open in late 2019 amidst general neighborhood approval.

Sadly, many houses of worship have been displaced over the years due to fires. Other than the massive losses associated with the 1906 disaster, some other major blazes have included fires at St. Mary's Cathedral (1962/demolished); Old St. Mary's Church (1966/restored 1967); Guerrero Street's Metropolitan Community Church (1973/relocated); Army Street's St. Anthony's Church (1975/demolished/rebuilt new 1977); Geary Street's former Beth Israel Synagogue, which had been repurposed as an art gallery (1989/demolished); St. Paulus Evangelical Lutheran Church (1995/demolished/under new construction 2019); and the Mission District's St. Peter's Church (1997/restored 2000).

St. Paulus Ev. Lutheran Church

Eddy and Gough Streets, San Francisco
Car No. 31 Direct — Car "H" to Eddy (2 blocks West)
G. E. KIRCHNER - Pastors - F. A. JACOBSEN
Parsonage: 969 Eddy Street, Phone ORdway 4183
The Pioneer Church of the Missouri Synod on the
Pacific Coast — Organized 1867.
Visitors and strangers are cordially invited to meet the Pastors
in the Narthex after services.

St. Paulus Lutheran Church, built from 1892 to 1894, was named a San Francisco landmark in 1980. It survived a serious fire in the 1940s and was repaired. Sadly, it was destroyed by a massive blaze in November 1995, with the site remaining vacant until it was announced in 2019 that a rebuilding program would commence on an apartment tower at the site and a smaller house of worship within the new structure. *Glenn D. Koch collection.*

San Francisco's Victorian homes, much loved and treasured today, suffered from a lack of respect, particularly in the post–World War II years. Other than outright demolition, other indignities included the installation of vinyl siding and aluminum-framed windows, removal of architectural details and overall lack of maintenance. Sadly, thousands of these homes were demolished in the 1940s, '50s and '60s.

Sporting venues have also come and gone—both physically and in name only.

Seals Stadium opened at 16th and Bryant Streets in 1931 for minor-league baseball and was used for that purpose until 1957; it was also home to the San Francisco Giants baseball team for their first two seasons on the West Coast—1958 and 1959. After Candlestick Park was dedicated

THE CALIFORNIA ARCHITECT/ BUILDING NEWS

ROUNTREE BRO'S. BLOCK.
COR. WASHINGTON & BUCHANAN ST'S.
W.H.LILLIE, ARCH'T. – RMS. 23–25 ST. ANN'S BLDG.

Many grand San Francisco homes such as these have fallen in the name of "progress." The post–World War II years were an especially difficult period for historic preservation. *Glenn D. Koch collection.*

in April 1960, Seals Stadium was demolished for a White Front discount department store. By the early 1980s, the site became home to several car dealers, and prior to the turn of the millennium, it became home to a multitenant shopping center. In a thoughtful nod to history, one of the stores, Office Depot, placed a large blue X on their floor to mark the exact spot where home plate once stood. Other than a popular nearby neighborhood watering hole, the Double Play, which is located just across the street, the excitement of baseball at Seals Stadium has been largely forgotten.

Kezar Stadium, built in 1925, was the home of numerous professional as well as scholastic football games as well as track and field and other sporting events. The 1928 high school football playoffs between rivals Polytechnic and Lowell drew more than fifty thousand fans—a record turnout for a high school football game in Northern California. With the move of major-league football games to the newer Candlestick Park in 1971, Kezar continued as a place for high school sports and also became a venue for many rock concerts.

The final NFL game at the old Kezar Stadium was held between the San Francisco 49ers and the Dallas Cowboys on January 3, 1971. The 49ers subsequently played at Candlestick Park until they left San Francisco for Levi's Stadium, located forty miles south in the city of Santa Clara, in 2014. *Author's collection.*

The original stadium was demolished in 1989 and replaced with a smaller (ten-thousand-seat) venue with the same name.

Candlestick Park opened in 1960, and critics were quick to point out some of its shortcomings almost up to the moment of its final demolition in 2015. From 1995 until 2002, naming rights were granted to 3Com Corporation, and the stadium was known as 3Com Park at Candlestick Point (or just 3Com Park). In 2002, the naming rights expired, and the site became known as San Francisco Stadium at Candlestick Point. In 2004, a new naming rights agreement was reached with Monster Cable, which renamed the site Monster Park. San Franciscans voted in November 2004 that the name would revert to Candlestick Park upon the expiration of the Monster agreement in 2008.

Over its fifty-five-year lifespan, the "Stick" was the site of numerous major-league baseball and football games, one college playoff game (Cal Bears vs. Fresno Bulldogs in 2011), the final public concert performed by the Beatles (1966), the only public Papal Mass in San Francisco history (celebrated by St. John Paul II in 1987) and a closing show hosted by Paul McCartney in 2014, after which the 49ers football team relocated to the new $1.3 billion Levi's Stadium some forty miles south in the city of Santa Clara.

History continues to evolve in the new millennium. Even before San Francisco's new forty-thousand-seat downtown ballpark opened in the spring of 2000, it was named Pacific Bell Park (often shorted to PacBell) for

Souvenir replica ticket from the final paid concert by the Beatles, which was held at Candlestick Park on August 29, 1966. *Author's collection.*

the local telecommunications firm. Following a 2003 corporate merger, the park's name was changed to SBC Park (SBC being the revised corporate name of a company once known as Southwestern Bell Communications upon its 1984 spin-off from AT&T). In 2006, after SBC acquired its one-time parent, AT&T, and took on that corporate name, the stadium was renamed AT&T Park. Most recently, in time for the 2019 baseball season, the site was renamed Oracle Park (which is separate and distinct from Oracle Arena in Oakland) as part of a multiyear naming-rights agreement.

Last—but certainly not least—are the more than five thousand union-built earthquake shacks that were constructed after the 1906 disaster and clustered into multiple camps. After 1907–08, many were moved and incorporated into newly built dwellings or simply demolished. These important components of local architectural history have been saved from extinction and now serve as a gentle reminder of local history.

This earthquake shack was restored by a group of volunteers from Western Neighborhoods Project and exhibited on Market Street for the 100th anniversary of the 1906 earthquake in 2006. It is now on permanent display at the San Francisco Zoo. *Western Neighborhoods Project.*

6

Modern School Days

I t's a given that when two San Franciscans meet for the first time, the first question that will be asked is: "Where'd you go to school?" Both speaker and listener clearly understand that the question refers to high school.

While the school mentioned is often Lowell, Lincoln, Washington, St. Ignatius, Sacred Heart, Riordan, Mercy or one of several others, there are many new choices today.

A dwindling school-age population has certainly heavily contributed to the many recent changes among both public and private schools in San Francisco. According to recent U.S. Census Bureau statistics, there are only about 115,000 children under the age of eighteen living in San Francisco. At the same time, San Francisco Animal Care and Control estimated there were about 120,000 to 150,000 dogs in the City. This ratio has been consistent for the last twenty years.

Declining enrollment also caused major changes in the past, including the 1950 closure of Commerce High School (with the bulldog as its mascot) on Van Ness Avenue and the shutdown of Polytechnic High School (the Parrots) on Frederick Street in the Inner Sunset after 1972.

Today, the San Francisco Unified School District (SFUSD) is the seventh-largest school district in California, educating 54,063 students (as of October 2017) in 136 schools. The district includes elementary schools (kindergarten through fifth grade), alternatively configured schools (kindergarten through eighth grade), middle schools (grades six through eight), high schools (grades nine through twelve), schools with Transitional Kindergarten (TK) and charter schools.

The thought-provoking banner displayed at a reunion at George Washington High School reads: "A time together, to be together, for we never know when we will see each other again." *Tammy Aramian photo/Artam Photography.*

Anza School welcomed students for the first time in 1952. In 1981, the building became Wallenberg High School. *San Francisco History Center/San Francisco Public Library.*

Public High Schools

Most people are familiar with San Francisco's large public high schools (Balboa, Galileo, Lincoln, Lowell, Mission and Washington), though there have been recent significant changes.

Abraham Lincoln: Opened in 1940 as the first public high school in the expanding Sunset District, Lincoln now occupies four full city blocks, and as a comprehensive high school, it is open to all residents of San Francisco. Having long since recovered from some performance challenges in earlier years, Lincoln is now the second-most-requested high school in the SFUSD after Lowell.

Balboa: Popularly known as "Bal" and founded in 1928, the present campus was completed in 1931—making it one of only two historic landmark public high school buildings in San Francisco (the other is Mission). Struggling with poor academic scores in the 1990s, the school district removed the entire staff just prior to the turn of the millennium and implemented a college prep curriculum. Today, Bal ranks third-highest in academic achievement among local public high schools, surpassed only by the Ruth Asawa School of the Arts (in second place) and Lowell (in first).

Galileo Academy of Science and Technology: Opened in the early 1920s, Galileo refocused its curriculum in the 1995–96 school year. With an emphasis on science and technology, the school offers a clear career path to students, with in-house specialties including the Galileo Health Academy, the Academy of Information Technology Biotechnology Pathway and the Environmental Science Pathway. Subsequent additions in the first decade of this millennium include the Publications Pathway, the Academy of Hospitality and Tourism and the Digital Photography Pathway.

Lowell: Founded in 1856 as the Union Grammar School, Lowell's current name was adopted in 1896. During fifty years of operation at Hayes Street and Masonic Avenue, the school developed a reputation as San Francisco's premier college preparatory public high school. Lowell, along with School of the Arts, has a competitive admission process for San Francisco residents and currently serves nearly 2,700 students at its Lake Merced campus, which opened in the fall of 1962.

Mission: Mission is the oldest San Francisco public high school still on its original site. Founded in 1890, and with a new building constructed at the present location in 1896, the school survived the 1906 earthquake and fire and served as a neighborhood shelter. It was rebuilt following a 1922 fire, with another full-scale renovation in the 1970s and yet another physical update currently underway. The school's offerings include an Academic Scholars Advancement Program that offers off-site summer enrichment opportunities to Mission students.

Philip and Sala Burton Academic High School: Opened in 1984 and now operating at the Mansell Street site of the former Woodrow Wilson High School (1963–96), the school now serves 1,300 students with a college prep curriculum. Student achievement on standardized testing has increased significantly in the past decade.

Raoul Wallenberg Traditional High School: Founded in 1981 and named for the Swedish diplomat, the school operates with more than 600 students on the remodeled campus of the former Anza School near Masonic Avenue. In the 2018–19 school year, the principal began holding monthly fireside chats with parents in the school's media center/library during late afternoon/early evening hours.

Ruth Asawa School of the Arts: In 1982, School of the Arts (SOTA) was established on the campus of J Eugene McAteer, though it was separate from the original high school. McAteer had been established in 1973 to replace Polytechnic High School, but by the late 1990s, McAteer began losing enrollment and experiencing a drop in graduation rates. SFUSD voted in early 2002 to close the thirty-year-old school at the end of that academic year. SOTA relocated when McAteer was under renovation, and in 2010, it returned to Portola Drive as Ruth Asawa San Francisco School of the Arts at the McAteer Campus, where it currently shares space with The Academy–San Francisco@McAteer.

Thurgood Marshall Academic High School: Founded in 1994 as a new academic college-prep high school, the campus occupies the former site of Pelton Junior High near Silver Avenue. The school operates a college and career center, with regular field trips for students to explore many nearby colleges and universities.

Washington: Opened in the Richmond District in 1936, the school now has an enrollment of 2,000 students and has been ranked among the top five hundred public high schools in the United States. The curriculum includes multiple Advanced Placement courses, and Washington is one of only two San Francisco public high schools with a marching band. The school also has programs in place to help students who have recently arrived in the United States and special-needs students, who comprise about 10 percent of the student body.

Reunion for George Washington High School graduates from the classes of 1970 through 1979, circa 2015. *Tammy Aramian photo/Artam Photography.*

In recent years, SFUSD has begun operating several smaller alternative high schools: Academy, City Arts and Tech, Civic Center Secondary, Downtown, Five Keys Independence, Gateway, Hilltop, Ida B. Wells, Independence, International Studies Academy, June Jordan School for Equity, Leadership, Life Learning Academy, San Francisco Flex Academy and San Francisco International.

PRIVATE SCHOOL/PUBLIC PURPOSE

In January 1895, the California School of Mechanical Arts—often referred to as "Lick" for its original financial benefactor James Lick, who donated $540,000 to endow the school—opened in San Francisco. It offered free education to both boys and girls with a curriculum that combined general intellectual preparation with technical and vocational instruction.

One year earlier, Jellis Wilmerding left $400,000 to the Regents of the University of California to fund the Wilmerding School of Industrial Arts—a school for boys specializing in building trades and architectural drafting. The Wilmerding School was located adjacent to the California School of Mechanical Arts, and the two institutions soon shared the services of George Merrill as director of each school.

Also in 1894, Miranda Lux, originally from Rhode Island and a longtime supporter of the San Francisco Protestant Orphan Asylum, died and left a significant bequest, directing to her executors: "It is my desire to assist in furnishing facilities for the education of young children in what is known as 'manual training' and all kinds of training by and through which habits of industry and practical knowledge of those things which are useful in earning a living may be acquired." The Lux School for Industrial Training for Girls began operating out of Lick's building before Lux built its own adjacent facilities. The curriculum was organized around five subjects: sewing and textiles, food, health, art and retailing/merchandising. Merrill, who was already managing both the Lick and Wilmerding schools, was also hired by the Lux trustees to manage their new school.

From the post-earthquake years until 1939, the three schools shared facilities and faculty at the 17th Street and Potrero Avenue site in the Mission District. Later, the institutions began operating in a more independent fashion. Lux closed down in the early 1950s, and its students transitioned into Lick, with Lux's assets and endowment moving into an entity known as the Lux Foundation, which continues to focus on the educational needs of children in San Francisco. Around the same time, California School of Mechanical Arts (Lick) and the Wilmerding School of Industrial Arts formally merged their operations, and in 1955, the school moved to a new campus on Ocean Avenue, rebranding itself as Lick-Wilmerding High School, which was a boys-only institution for seventeen years, until returning to coed status in 1972.

The school aptly describes itself as such: "a private school with public purpose, Lick-Wilmerding High School develops the head, heart, and hands of highly motivated students from all walks of life, inspiring them to become lifelong learners who contribute to the world with confidence and compassion."

Today, Lick-Wilmerding is a fully coeducational college preparatory institution with nearly 500 students from more than one hundred different middle schools. Each year, the school receives 900 applications for the 125 seats in the incoming ninth-grade class. There is a high level of ethnic diversity, with nearly 60 percent of the students self-identifying as a background/ethnicity other than Caucasian, including 26 percent who categorize themselves as multiracial.

Based on the early endowment funds from the Lick, Wilmerding and Lux trusts (nearly $15 million in today's dollars), the three schools have long been able to offer a tuition-free education to students—a practice that continued even after the merger and the 1955 move to Ocean Avenue. By the mid-1970s, however, costs had risen to the point that a tuition program had to be introduced, though with endowment funds subsidizing the cost based on a student's family circumstances. Today, the program is known as Flexible Tuition, with parents paying as little as $1,000 per school year based on a sliding scale and demonstrated financial need. Nearly 40 percent of current students qualify for Flexible Tuition, with the full annual amount now set at $42,500.

Admission to Lick-Wilmerding involves a multistep application process:

- Initial inquiry
- Campus "shadow" visit
- Open house
- Standardized test
- Parent/guardian application
- Student application
- Student interview
- Recommendations from middle school principal/teachers
- Submission of official middle school transcript

Lick-Wilmerding has long required students to take an entrance exam for admission, and in the 1960s, that test was scheduled several weeks in advance of similar tests for admission to San Francisco's boys' Catholic high schools. This author and many of his St. Cecilia School classmates were in Lick's gymnasium taking the Lick entrance exam as practice on a cold Saturday morning back in January 1966 for a modest five-dollar fee—and just for the record, I PASSED!

Remaining faithful to its century-old history as a pioneering institution in the technical arts, LWHS offers a unique collection of shop classes, including a basic understanding of the qualities and characteristics of materials in the glass, electronics, machine, jewelry and wood shops. Other courses serve to foster an appreciation of the design principles first introduced in the drafting and design courses.

Campus facilities have been expanded and improved since the Ocean Avenue campus opened in 1955, including the technical arts shops, cafeteria, full-court gymnasium with rock climbing wall, music studio, dance studio, photography studio with darkroom, three computer labs and a thirty-thousand-volume library. The school maintains a partnership with the adjacent City College of San Francisco for the use of their classrooms,

Architectural rendering of 2019 renovation/expansion project at Lick-Wilmerding High School. *Eleanor Sananman, Lick-Wilmerding High School.*

laboratories and sports facilities. Among the seventy-five faculty members employed by Lick-Wilmerding, the vast majority possess master's degrees, while eight have earned their doctorates.

The school's sports teams are known as the Tigers, and nearly 75 percent of Lick-Wilmerding students participate in one or more team sports—with a total of fifteen teams from which to choose. There are also more than forty student-led groups and organizations, including an extensive music program. In 2014, it was reported that Lick-Wilmerding students achieved the eighth highest SAT scores in the United States. As a college prep institution, virtually all graduates continue their educations beyond high school, and members of recent classes have been accepted at more than seventy-five different colleges and universities.

Today, Lick-Wilmerding grads go on to enjoy a variety of careers in engineering, architecture, technology and the fine arts. The school continues

to build its endowment, and in keeping with the noble aspirations of founders James Lick, Jellis Wilmerding and Miranda Lux, alumni have been very generous in donating to the school that helped them on their own personal paths to success.

Go Tigers!

OTHER PRIVATE SCHOOLS

There are 109 private schools in San Francisco serving 25,643 students. Approximately 50 percent of these schools have a religious affiliation, most often Jewish, Lutheran or Roman Catholic. Students of color represent 56 percent of enrollments in these schools, and all are coeducational except as noted below. Annual tuitions range from about $8,000 to $40,000 per student, with financial aid (and/or sliding-scale/flex tuition) often covering between 25 and 40 percent of students. Today, there are many private schools operating with more than 100 students each:

Adda Clevenger School (122 students) is an independent school for the arts that opened in 1980 and serves students in grades one through eight, with TK/K added more recently. The school operates in the former St. James Boys' School building in the Mission.

Bay School (346 students) serves students in grades nine through twelve and has been operating in the Presidio since 2004.

Brandeis School (400 students) is a K–8 private Jewish day school founded in 1963 and operating on Brotherhood Way.

Cathedral School for Boys (265 students) is a K–8 institution founded in 1957 and is affiliated with Grace Cathedral (Episcopal).

Children's Day School (440 students) is a pre-K–8 school located on Dolores Street. Opened in 1983, the school has more than doubled in size since then.

Chinese-American International School (520 students) opened in 1981 and now operates as a K–8 at three locations.

Cornerstone Academy (924 students) opened as a preschool on Lawton Street in 1975 and is now a pre-K–8 operating on three campus sites, including the old Simpson Bible College building on Silver Avenue.

Drew School (280 students) is an independent college-prep high school that has been operating at its current site on California Street since 1911, with a significant campus expansion in 2001.

French-American International School (1,100 students) is a pre-K–12 school founded in 1963 and operating in the Civic Center neighborhood.

Hamlin School (404 students) is a private K–8 girls' school established by Sarah Dix Hamlin in 1898, with roots going back to 1863.

Jewish Community High School (153 students) was founded in 2001 and now serves students in grades nine through twelve at its Western Addition neighborhood site.

Katherine Delmar Burke (402 students) is a private K–8 girls' school in the Sea Cliff neighborhood. Founded in Pacific Heights in 1908, the school included a high school division until 1975.

KZV Armenian School (122 students) was established in 1980 as a pre-K–1 school on Brotherhood Way, with additional grade levels added annually until it became K–8.

Lisa Kampner Hebrew Academy (107 students) opened as a pre-K–3 school in the Richmond District in 1969, later expanding to K–12, and graduated its first high school class in 1980.

Live Oak School (266 students) was established in 1971 as a K–5 school and expanded to K–8 in 1992. The school now operates on Potrero Hill.

Lycée Français de San Francisco (1,000 students) was founded in 1967 and operates pre-K–5 at the old St. Agnes School on Ashbury Street (acquired in 1996), and grades 6–12 at the former San Francisco Conservatory of Music (acquired in 2005) on 19th Avenue.

Marin Preparatory Academy (200 students) is a TK–5 school founded in 2008 and currently operating at the site of the former Most Holy Redeemer School in the Castro.

Presidio Hill (200 students) is the oldest K–8 progressive school in California, established in 1918 and operating in Pacific Heights.

Presidio Knolls (207 students) was founded in 2008 as a Mandarin-language immersion school operating at the old St. Joseph School site South-of-Market.

San Francisco Day School (396 students) began in 1981 as a private K–2 school and expanded to K–12 after acquiring/remodeling the former Carew & English Mortuary at Golden Gate and Masonic Avenues in 1985.

San Francisco Friends School (400 students) is located in the Mission District and began operating in 2002, following traditional Quaker teachings.

San Francisco School (275 students) was founded in 1966 as a Montessori school in the Portola neighborhood and is now K–8, with two classes at each grade level.

Stratford School (300 students) was founded in 1999 and operates as a K–8 school at three sites, including the former Corpus Christi and St. Emydius schools.

Sterne School (158 students) was established in 1976 for students in grades four through eight who were not finding success in regular classrooms and now operates from the former site of St. Mary's School.

Town School for Boys (400 students) is a K–8 school in Pacific Heights founded in 1939 with two classes per grade level.

University High School (410 students) is a college-prep school established in the 1970s in Pacific Heights, with numerous expansions over the years.

The Urban School (420 students) is a college-prep school founded in 1966 and operating at two sites in the Haight-Ashbury neighborhood.

Waldorf School (462 students) operates as pre-K–12 at two sites: a grade school in Pacific Heights and a high school on West Portal Avenue at Sloat Boulevard.

West Portal Lutheran (500 students) was founded in 1951 and now has two campus sites: grades K–3 at 37th Avenue and Moraga (site acquired in 1974 and later rebuilt) and grades 4–8 at the original 19th Avenue and Sloat site.

Zion Lutheran (153 students) is a K–8 school that has been operating in the Richmond District since 1947.

CATHOLIC SCHOOLS

Long gone are the days when nuns singlehandedly ran classrooms with 50-plus students and tuition was $6 per month, *per family.* Today, there are only a handful of nuns still serving as teachers or administrators throughout the entire city. Many Catholic elementary schools in the central and eastern parts of San Francisco have closed or merged, while schools in the Richmond and Sunset districts that once served 500 to 800-plus students each now have enrollments that are half that. Annual tuition in most local K–8 Catholic schools is about $8,000 (often $20,000-plus at the high school level), with up to 50 percent of students receiving sliding-scale discounts for multiple siblings/financial need. More than half the students in Catholic schools today are identified by their families as children of color.

There are twenty-eight Catholic elementary schools operating in San Francisco today. Teachers (mostly lay women and men) have bachelor's degrees and California teaching credentials, and many also possess master's degrees. The presence of even a single nun, priest or brother on a school's faculty is rare today.

Schools accept Catholic and non-Catholic students, offer financial aid and are open to all—traditional "parish boundaries" are no longer enforced. Most schools include classroom aides, counselors, learning specialists, tech staff, music teachers, religious coordinators and physical education instructors, plus science and computer labs. Many offer extended-care after-school programs for an additional fee, several are introducing Transitional Kindergarten programs and all are coed except as noted. [Author's note: The *Archdiocese of San Francisco 2019 Official Directory* does not report enrollment numbers for individual elementary schools, so the figures shown here had to be obtained from school/parish websites where available.]

Convent of the Sacred Heart: K–8 school for girls headquartered in the former Flood Mansion at 2222 Broadway, and part of Schools of the Sacred Heart, tracing its San Francisco origin to 1887.

De Marillac Academy: Opened in 2001 in the Tenderloin neighborhood adjacent to St. Boniface Church, the school provides tuition-free education to more than 100 students in grades 4–8.

Ecole Notre Dame des Victoires: Founded in 1924 adjacent to its namesake church on Bush Street, the K–8 school serves 300 students with daily instruction in the French language.

Epiphany: Opened in 1938 and originally staffed by the Sisters of the Presentation, the school quickly expanded, and by 1948, it had become one of many local Catholic elementary schools with two classes per grade level—and it still maintains that distinction, with 400-plus students in grades K–8.

Father Sauer Academy: Opened at St. Ignatius College Prep in 2017 as a tuition-free middle school for high-achieving sixth-grade girls and boys from underserved communities, it is expanding to 90 students (grades 6–8) by the fall of 2019.

Holy Name: Opened in the Sunset District in 1941 as a K–8 school with Sisters of Mercy and, later, Canossian Sisters. Today it serves 315 students with a lay faculty. A preschool was added in 2012.

Mission Dolores Academy: Formed by the 2011 merger of Megan Furth Catholic Academy (itself formed by a 2003 consolidation of two Western Addition schools, Sacred Heart and St. Dominic) with Mission Dolores School to form the new academy. According to the academy's website: "The school's history stretches as far back as 1852, making it the longest standing Catholic school in San Francisco."

Our Lady of the Visitacion: One of San Francisco's newer parochial schools, Our Lady of the Visitacion opened in 1963 in a parish that traces its origin to 1907. Today, the K–8 school serves 267 students.

SS. Peter & Paul: Established in North Beach in 1925, the school now serves 247 students in grades K–8 and has been under the direction of the Daughters of Mary Help of Christians since 1950. The school offers language lessons in both Spanish and Italian beginning in kindergarten.

St. Anne of the Sunset: Established in 1920, the pre-K–8 school offers traditional instruction plus language classes in Cantonese and Mandarin. In 2017, it became the first local Catholic elementary school to complete required seismic/access retrofits.

St. Anthony–Immaculate Conception: This school was formed by the 2002 merger of two Mission District Catholic elementary schools.

St. Brendan: Opened in 1947 with 241 students and a staff of Dominican sisters, the school reached its peak enrollment in the 1950s with 438 students. Today, it serves 321 students with an all-lay faculty.

St. Brigid: Founded in 1888 and staffed by Sisters of Charity of the Blessed Virgin Mary, then Sisters of Mercy of Dublin, Ireland (1970–1982). Today, the Sisters of the Immaculate Conception from Madrid, Spain, serve with a lay faculty. Since the 1994 closing of St. Brigid Church, the pre-K–8 school has conducted religious services at St. Mary's Cathedral.

St. Cecilia: Opened in 1930 and now San Francisco's largest Catholic elementary school, with two classes per grade level (today's head count is 618 vs. 880 in the mid-1950s). There is a seismic/access upgrade program underway, and the school added a Transitional Kindergarten program in the renovated convent in the fall of 2018.

St. Finn Barr: Established in 1962 and staffed by Irish Sisters of Mercy until 1997, then by the Dominican Sisters of the Most Holy Rosary of the Philippines until 2003. Today, the school has a lay faculty serving 248 students in grades K–8.

St. Gabriel: Founded in 1948, the school grew to become the largest Catholic elementary school west of Chicago by the 1950s, with three classes of 50 students at each grade level for a total enrollment of 1,200. Today, the school serves 500 students, with two classes per grade level, with the lower grades at one class per grade level since the 2018–19 school year.

St. James: This longtime Mission District school opened in 1924 and has roots going back to the late 1800s. It is now serving about 200 students in grades K–8.

St. John: Founded in 1917 in the Glen Park/Mission Terrace neighborhood, the school now serves 228 students in grades K–8.

St. Monica: Operating since 1919 in the Richmond District, the school serves about 225 students today in grades K–8. As part of a 2017 merger of St. Monica/St. Thomas the Apostle parishes, each school maintains a separate identity.

St. Paul: Established in 1916, St. Paul School was once the largest Catholic elementary school west of Chicago, with 1,000 students until the 1950s, when St. Gabriel in the Sunset District expanded to 1,200 students. As part of a 1994–98 seismic retrofit, St. Paul constructed a new facility and has been operating there since 1999. The school currently serves 214 students in grades K–8.

St. Peter: Operating in the Mission District since 1878, St. Peter School now serves 250-plus students in a modern facility built around 1960. The school has an active alumni association that provides significant financial assistance to families of students.

St. Philip: Opened in 1938, St. Philip School now serves 259 students in grades Pre-K–8, a reflection of many families with children now living in Noe Valley. The school responded to parent requests and established a pre-K program in 2005.

St. Stephen: Opened in 1952, shortly after the founding of the parish, the school began with 164 students in grades 1–6. Today, it serves 306 students in grades K–8, with a new wing completed in the year 2000. The school began offering after-school programs over thirty years ago.

St. Thomas More: Located adjacent to the Parkmerced community, the school opened in the 1950s as part of a new parish and today serves 300 students in grades pre-K–8.

St. Thomas the Apostle: Richmond District school that currently serves 300 students in grades pre-K–8. The school has offered language classes in Mandarin and Cantonese for twenty years, and like many local schools, it is in the midst of a seismic/access retrofit program. As part of the 2017 merger of St. Monica and St. Thomas the Apostle parishes, each school maintains a separate identity.

St. Vincent dePaul: Opened in 1924 in the Marina/Cow Hollow/Pacific Heights neighborhood, the school expanded to a second building in the years after World War II and today serves 265 students in grades K–8.

Stuart Hall: Founded in 1956 as a male counterpart to the girls-only Convent of the Sacred Heart, this K–8 school has an enrollment of 200 boys.

Twenty Catholic elementary schools have closed or merged because of declining enrollment numbers since the World War II era—half of them in this millennium. The Diocese of Oakland has experienced similar challenges, closing five of their elementary schools in 2017 alone.

All Hallows School (Bayview): Closed in the 1980s.

Convent of the Good Shepherd (Bayview): Founded in 1932 to serve girls involved with the justice system, the school's focus changed in 2010 to that of a licensed recovery residence for adult women.

Corpus Christi (Excelsior): Closed in 2011.

Morning Star (Western Addition): Closed in the 1990s.

Most Holy Redeemer (Castro): Closed in the 1990s.

Sacred Heart (Western Addition): Merged with St. Dominic to become Megan Furth Catholic Academy in 2003, operating in the former St. Dominic School building at Pine and Steiner. In 2011, Megan Furth Academy merged with Mission Dolores School to become Mission Dolores Academy, operating at 16th and Church Streets.

St. Agnes (Haight-Ashbury): Closed in 1996.

St. Boniface School (Tenderloin): Closed in the 1960s.

St. Charles (Mission): Closed in 2017.

St. Dominic (Western Addition): Merged with Sacred Heart in 2003.

St. Elizabeth (Portola): Closed in 2010.

St. Emydius (Ingleside): Closed in 2003.
St. James Boys' (Mission): Merged with St. James Girls' in the 1970s.
St. Joan of Arc (Hunters Point): Closed in the 1950s.
St. Joseph (10th and Howard): Closed in the 1980s.
St. Mary (Chinatown): Closed in 2016.
St. Michael (Oceanview): Closed in the 1980s.
St. Patrick (South-of-Market): Closed in the early 1960s.
St. Paul of the Shipwreck (Bayview): Closed in 2003.
St. Teresa (Potrero Hill): Closed in the 1980s.
Star of the Sea Elementary (Richmond District): Closed in June 2019 after 110 years in operation.

St. Ignatius High School, 222 Stanyan Street, third floor, looking north, spring of 1969. The building, opened in 1929, had been serving S.I. for forty years and was attended by more than 7,500 students. In 1969, the school moved to 37th Avenue in the Sunset District. Sold to the adjacent University of San Francisco, the Stanyan Street building was then used by USF as classroom space until 1987, when it was demolished to make room for a new college recreational facility. *John Martini photo.*

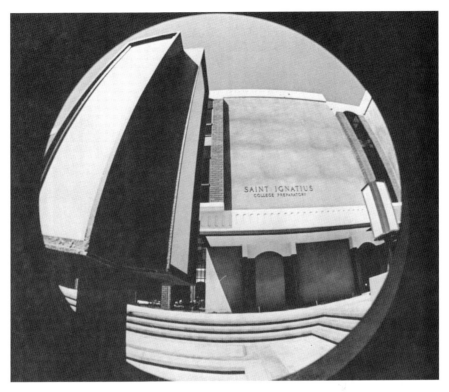

St. Ignatius High School was renamed St. Ignatius College Preparatory when it made the move to 37th Avenue in August 1969. The school became coed in 1989, and more students have graduated from this campus over the last fifty years than from all of S.I.'s previous campus locations (1855 through 1969) combined. *Keith Forner photo.*

As of 2019, there are seven Catholic high schools operating in San Francisco:

Archbishop Riordan: Opened in 1949, the school is one of two boys-only Catholic high schools in San Francisco and serves about 700 students. It initiated a boarding program in 2011 for students from overseas and has recently begun offering a four-year honors engineering program.

Convent of the Sacred Heart: Part of the Schools of the Sacred Heart, Convent is one of three girls-only Catholic high schools in San Francisco and operates at the old Flood Mansion on Broadway with about 200 students.

ICA–Christo Rey Academy: Formerly known as Immaculate Conception Academy, admission is now limited to girls from low-income households with a four-year work-study program.

Mercy: Founded in 1952, it remains one of three girls-only Catholic high schools. From 1956 to 1990, Mercy's enrollment was about 800 girls (200 per grade level), but when Sacred Heart Cathedral and St. Ignatius went coed (in 1987 and 1989, respectively), Catholic coeducation became a new option. Mercy's head count soon settled at 400 total—100 per grade level. The 2019 graduating class included 86 graduates, and the incoming ninth-grade class in 2018 consisted of 55 students.

Sacred Heart Cathedral: Cathedral High School (girls) and Sacred Heart High School (boys) merged in 1987, and today, the school currently serves 1,300-plus students.

St. Ignatius: Founded in 1855 on Market Street, the school, coed since 1989, will celebrate fifty years in the Sunset District in 2019 and currently serves 1,485 students.

Stuart Hall: This all-male Catholic high school opened in 2000 as counterpart to the all-female Convent of the Sacred Heart with an enrollment of 200 students.

The following Catholic high schools have closed since the World War II era:

Notre Dame de Namur (**Dolores Street**): Closed in 1981.
Notre Dame des Victoires (**Bush Street**): Closed in 1970.
Presentation (**Turk Street**): Closed in 1991.
St. Brigid (**Van Ness Avenue**): Closed in the 1950s.
St. Charles Commercial (**Mission District**): Closed before World War II.
St. James (**Mission District**): Closed in 1949 when its successor school, Archbishop Riordan High School, opened.
St. John Ursuline (**Mission Street**): Closed in 1990.
St. Paul (**Church Street**): Closed in 1994.
St. Peter Girls' (**Mission District**): Closed in 1966.
St. Peter Boys' (**Mission District**): Closed after World War II.
St. Rose (**Pine Street**): Closed in 1990.
St. Vincent (**Geary and Gough**): Closed in the 1960s and reemerged as Cathedral High, which later merged with nearby Sacred Heart in 1987 to form Sacred Heart Cathedral Prep.
Star of the Sea (**9th Avenue**): Closed in 1985.

An ongoing decline in San Francisco's population of school-age children, plus increasing operational costs, will surely lead to more changes in the years ahead.

7
Signs of the Times

G rowing up in San Francisco, everyone was accustomed to seeing numerous iconic business signs all around town. These were classic markers that often resonated in the minds of viewers. While many of them have quietly vanished over the years, several are still here and sparking nostalgic thoughts. Think back for just a moment to some of the memorable signs from another era…

In an earlier time, whenever our family was coming home from a visit to Oakland or other points east, there were bright red lights on the bay-facing side of the Ferry Buildings reading "Port Of San Francisco" to greet us. We were home, and on the lookout for other familiar icons—neon, metal, plastic—to remind us of exactly where we were.

As we approached the west end of the Bay Bridge, there was the bright orange Union 76 logo atop a tower at the firm's headquarters on Rincon Hill. Grandma always took the time to remind us that when she and my grandfather were children in the late nineteenth century, they grew up near there, walking, playing and going to school in a neighborhood that was still heavily residential in the days before 1906.

Continuing westward, we saw the enormous brilliant red neon Coca-Cola sign and, later, the sparkling Hamm's Beer sign, with yellow and white lights representing beer filling the glass, then cascading over the sides again and again.

Then there were times that Dad would pick all of us up after a shopping trip downtown. He always liked to show us where he began working for the

The classic Hamm's Brewery sign, located at 1550 Bryant Street, was visible from many parts of the City, including seats at nearby Seals Stadium. Yellow and white lights made the glass appear to fill with beer that cascaded over the rim and down the sides. *Robert W. Skelton Photography/Judy Skelton.*

post office in the days before World War II—the Rincon Annex Post Office with its simple period lettering and images of dolphins above the entrances. Heading back to Market Street, we could see the giant letters "S.P." (for Southern Pacific railroad), which were removed by the company in the 1950s in order to improve the scenery. At Market and Montgomery, there was a rooftop sign featuring plain lighted letters that simply read "THE PALACE," with no further description necessary.

Heading west on Market Street, we spotted the familiar sign of The Emporium, one of downtown's most popular destinations for young and old. Beneath the great glass dome, there were four sales floors plus a bargain basement selling everything "from a needle to an anchor." Just beyond, there was the five-story-tall "PENNEY'S" sign at the corner of 5th Street, and a few doors farther west, an equally tall sign in red neon: "KRESS."

Continuing along Market Street, we were soon in the incredible world of neon that marked several blocks of movie theatres. From the old State at 4th and Market (later demolished for a new Roos-Atkins store in the late 1960s and now a bland office building), we could see the marquees stretching out in front of us—Newsreel, United Artists, Paramount, Orpheum and dozens of others—all the way to the granddaddy of them all, the Fox, with its massive vertical sign. Sadly, as BART construction was underway, the Board of Supervisors rewrote the rules about the use of neon in Market Street signage. Today, the few theatres that survive do not convey the same sense of excitement that we once felt.

The iconic sign from the front wall at 835 Market Street remains in place even though the store itself closed in 1995 after ninety-nine years in business. *Anne Evers Hitz photo.*

As we motored west toward Twin Peaks, there were hundreds of more brightly lighted signs for everything from painless dentistry to low-cost loans, plus cafés and bars of every kind, often marked by bright neon stemmed cocktail glasses with a toothpick and a cherry. The Hibernia Bank at 1 Jones Street projected its name with significant brass signs at the foot of its entrance stairway, plus some subtle, 1950s green neon letters above. Approaching Octavia Street (which marked the path of the Central Freeway from the 1950s through the 1990s), we would be on the lookout for the large, revolving See's Candy sign, which was shaped like a television set, on the roof of the company's now long-gone building at that intersection.

Soon, the big Safeway sign at Duboce Avenue, in place since about 1954, came into view. This marked the spot where we might turn if we were going to stop in and say hello to any one of Mom's or Dad's aunts and uncles who lived nearby. At Church Street, there was Burke's Drive-In—a favorite Saturday spot for hamburgers and milkshakes in an era when there were no McDonald's or other "fast food" outlets operating in San Francisco. At Castro Street, there was the enormous "BANK OF AMERICA" rooftop sign atop the bank's longtime office (prior to a name change in 1930, the sign used to read "BANK OF ITALY" in equally large letters), though city planners were able to persuade the bank to remove it by the early 1980s in favor of a much smaller sign as part of MUNI Metro's street beautification plans, while the adjacent Castro Theatre sign remains a bright red neighborhood landmark and beacon.

As we motored over Twin Peaks, there used to be dozens of lighted billboards on those first few blocks west of Castro, prompting youngsters to read them aloud in order to demonstrate recently acquired skills.

Even within our own Western Neighborhoods, we might be passing by the iconic Zim's, opened in 1957 at the corner of 19th Avenue, with large plate-glass windows and red neon proclaiming the restaurant's name and the words "Broiled Hamburgers." Just a few doors away was one of the

Above: The classic art deco Ocean Park Motel has been holding down the northeast corner of 46th Avenue and Wawona Street since 1937, when it opened as San Francisco's first motel, coinciding with the completion of the Golden Gate Bridge. The quiet, homey atmosphere makes it a popular spot with tourists—especially returning visitors who were once local residents. *Al Barna and Randall Ann Holman/SF Neon.*

Left: Doggie Diner was a local fast-food chain long before the big firms arrived. A restored dachshund head that once stood at a nearby outlet of the firm was dedicated as a piece of street art on Sloat Boulevard near the zoo in 2001 and has since been given Designated Landmark status. *Alvis Hendley photo/Noe Hill collection.*

neighborhood's other memorable signs on the Parkside Theatre, with its large red marquee reflected in the foggy nighttime mist for blocks. Various other neighborhood businesses also announced their presence in rainbow hues, including the huge red script letter "E" on the side of the Emporium-Stonestown, the classic Ocean Park Motel near the zoo and the brightly lit Doggie Diner head at all of their outlets, including the one near Ocean Beach.

Movie houses were always known for their bright lights, but the El Rey on Ocean Avenue was unique because of the building's tower that continues to stand as a neighborhood beacon ninety years later.

Van Ness Avenue, the once-bustling auto row, used to display massive quantities of neon, plus aerial searchlights as new vehicle models were introduced early each fall. Today, there are no dealers selling new American-made cars anywhere in San Francisco, and the remaining new auto showrooms display much more subdued signage.

The revolving rooftop sign of the old Jack Tar Hotel at Van Ness and Geary was instantly recognizable from the time of its installation in 1960 until the hotel underwent a name change to Cathedral Hill Hotel in 1982 (the building was demolished in late 2013 and replaced by a new state-of-the-art hospital in early 2019). Farther along, on the opposite side of the street, there still remains a bit of classic red-and-white neon at House of Prime Rib.

Neon and twinkling bulbs were falling out of favor in other areas, too. Well-known landmarks that were once marked by bright lights included Folger's Coffee near the Embarcadero and the Planters Peanut Factory in the Bayview. Until the closure of the Fosters cafeteria chain in 1969, these outlets in many parts of San Francisco were brightly marked by red neon lettering often displayed against a background of black tile with a yellow horizontal stripe.

The Richmond District, with its many movie houses and neighborhood merchants, was an area of iconic signage long after memorable signs had faded from other areas. From the lighted shops of Laurel Village along California Street to businesses along Inner Clement and Balboa, all the way to outer Point Lobos, with the iconic signage of Sutro's and the Cliff House, memorable visual markers confirmed exactly where you were in the neighborhood.

Other longtime neon signs still in use today include those of St. Francis Fountain on 24th Street in the Mission, Tadich Grill in the Financial District, the Old Clam House on Bayshore Boulevard and the adjacent Alioto's and Fisherman's Grotto (No. 8 and No. 9, respectively) at Fisherman's Wharf.

Opening night advertisement for the El Rey Theatre, 1931. *Western Neighborhoods Project.*

Liguria Bakery on Stockton Street in North Beach has been in business since 1911 and is still selling the world's best focaccia. *Original artwork by Elizabeth Ashcroft (used with permission).*

In North Beach, the intersection of Broadway and Columbus was long dominated by a bigger-than-life image of dancer Carol Doda with strategically placed blinking red lights, while just a few blocks away, Liguria Bakery has continued to draw people in for more than one hundred years with simple gold lettering on a plate-glass window.

Downtown's City of Paris at Stockton and Geary included a mini Eiffel Tower on the roof, while John's Grill on nearby Ellis boasted the neon words "Steaks, Seafood, Cocktails" along with a reminder about the site's history: "Since 1908." Just a block away along the cable car line was Bernstein's Fish Grotto, with the prow of a wooden ship jutting out into Powell Street, and the bright red lettering on Woolworth's. Other retailers, such as W&J Sloan and Gump's, both specializing in home furnishings, were marked by solid metal signs at the entrances, while Podesta-Baldocchi on nearby

Above: John's Grill on Ellis Street, adjacent to the Flood Building, continues to serve excellent, simple fare in an old-time San Francisco atmosphere, just as it did in the late 1920s, when *Maltese Falcon* author Dashiell Hammett, who was living nearby on Post Street, was a regular patron. *Tammy Aramian photo/ Artam Photography.*

Left: The iconic Eiffel Tower sign atop City of Paris was a familiar sight to downtown shoppers for decades until the store closed in 1972. *OpenSFHistory.*

Gump's, San Francisco's classic store for home furnishings, china, crystal, silver, gifts and collectibles, was in business from 1861 until 2018. *Courtesy of a private collector.*

Sutter Street acquired a splash of neon in the 1950s, announcing its name in flowing red-and-white script along with the words "Flowers, Plants, Gifts."

Still, for many of us who lived, worked and shopped in downtown San Francisco when the green-and-cream MUNI streetcars ran on the surface of Market Street, one of the most welcome signs of all was the soft yellow glow from the destination marker on an approaching J–K–L–M–N streetcar bound for your neighborhood at the end of a long day.

Few parades in San Francisco history have matched the size of the event held to welcome home World War I troops in April 1919. This image shows Market Street looking east toward 6th Street. *Glenn D. Koch collection.*

8

We Love a Parade

The 1930s-era hit song "I Love a Parade" still resonates far and wide, especially in San Francisco, where numerous events dot the calendar each and every year—some are unique honors, such as the arrival of the New York Giants baseball team in San Francisco in 1958, a visit from French president Charles de Gaulle in 1960 or the massive celebrations of five 49ers Super Bowl wins in the 1980s and 1990s, plus events to honor the Giants baseball team following World Series victories in 2010, 2012 and 2014.

Here are just a few of the hundreds of activities—including parades, fairs, festivals and other events both established and new—that consistently draw large and appreciative crowds.

January

Martin Luther King Jr. Day march/parade

February

Chinese New Year parade
Tulipmania in Union Square

March

San Francisco History Days at the Old Mint
St. Patrick's Day parade

A Miss Chinatown contestant rides in the Chinese New Year parade on Market Street, 1965. *OpenSFHistory.*

April

Bay Area Dance Week
Cesar Chavez Festival and Parade
Earth Day
Earthquake Celebration
Glen Park Festival
International Film Festival
Japantown Cherry Blossom Festival
Mount Davidson Cross Annual Lighting
Union Street Easter parade/spring celebration

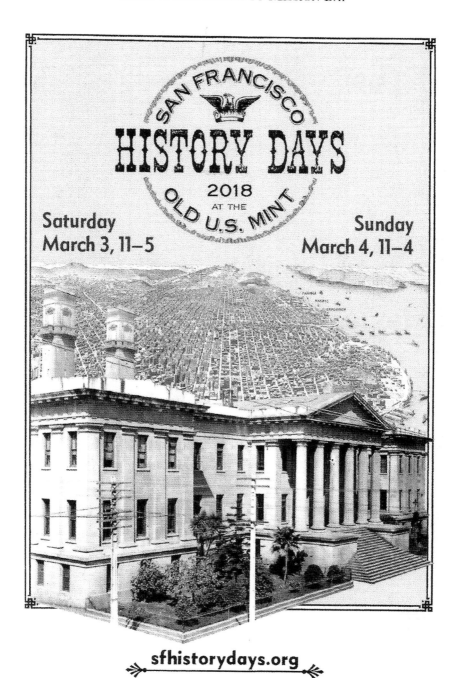

San Francisco History Days is a free annual event open to the public and held at the Old U.S. Mint. *Author's collection.*

May

Bay to Breakers Run
Carnaval
Cinco de Mayo
Memorial Day commemoration in Presidio
Taiwanese American Cultural Festival
Taste of Potrero

June

Haight Street Fair
Juneteenth
North Beach Festival
Pride

San Francisco Pride is an annual event held on the last Sunday in June since 1971. *Victor Grigas photo/ Wikimedia Commons.*

July

Fillmore Jazz Festival
Fourth of July Fireworks at Pier 39

August

Festival of the Sea
Nihonmachi Street Fair in Japantown
Outside Lands Music and Arts Festival
Polk Street Blues Festival

September

Chinatown Mid-Autumn Moon Festival
Folsom Street Fair
Ghirardelli Chocolate Festival
Taste of Greece

October

Castro Street Fair
Excelsior Arts and Music Festival
Fleet Week
Hardly Strictly Bluegrass Festival
Italian Heritage parade
San Francisco Old Car Picnic
Oktoberfest

November

Dia de los Muertos (Day of the Dead)
Fort Mason Craft Festival
Lighting of Union Square Christmas tree
Veterans' Day parade

October 13-17
1983

Left: San Francisco Fleet Week began in 1981 and soon became an annual event featuring numerous ceremonies and festivities. *Author's collection.*

Below: The San Francisco Italian Athletic Club, located near SS. Peter & Paul's Church in North Beach, has been the site of countless receptions after baptisms, weddings and funerals. In 2017, the club celebrated its centennial. *San Francisco Italian Athletic Club.*

Women's Army Corps members marching west on Market Street (at 3rd & Kearny Streets) in 1948. *OpenSFHistory.*

December

Ghirardelli Square tree lighting
Great Dickens Christmas Fair
Lighted Boat Holiday Parade
Living Nativity Scene–Knights of St. Francis
Union Square Hanukkah/Christmas lighting

Prior to the dawn of malls, big-box stores and online retailers, San Franciscans came together to fulfill many of their shopping needs downtown, as shown in this busy pedestrian scene at 5th and Market Streets in 1955. *San Francisco History Center/San Francisco Public Library.*

9
The Workday Routine

I t has been a very long time since businesses like Bank of America, Emporium, Union Iron Works, AT&T and Continental Can and industries like railroads and shipping were among San Francisco's largest employers. By the 1950s, tourism was becoming a big business as some older industries were beginning to fade. As this shift continued over the next few decades, hotels, restaurants and various small retailers serving visitors began to greatly expand.

The *San Francisco Business Times* recently ranked the City's ten largest employers (not including government agencies) by size in terms of the number of employees working in San Francisco:

Wells Fargo: 8,000-plus
Salesforce: 6,600
California Pacific Medical Center: 6,000
PG&E: 4,325
GAP: 4,268
Kaiser Permanente: 4,100
Uber: 3,650
Dignity Health: 2,500
Academy of Art University: 2,400
Williams-Sonoma: 2,200

According to a 2016 article in the *San Francisco Chronicle*, the City and County of San Francisco had more than 30,600 employees, with a projected increase of several hundred per year thereafter.

University of California–San Francisco (often referred to as UC-Med) boasts 24,000-plus employees, with campuses at Parnassus, Laurel Heights and Mission Bay. San Francisco State University has more than 3,600 faculty and staff. University of San Francisco has nearly 2,300 faculty and staff.

The federal government—with multiple office buildings, additional leased space in multiple locations and staff employed by the National Park Service and in work-from-home locations—employs tens of thousands more workers.

Many businesses with close ties to San Francisco now maintain headquarters and/or major facilities in other locations—even Rice-a-Roni, "the San Francisco Treat," is produced and distributed by Quaker Oats (a division of PepsiCo) in Chicago, Illinois. The following businesses have also relocated to areas outside of San Francisco (all cities located in California unless otherwise noted):

AAA Auto Club: Emeryville
Bank of America: Headquarters have been in Charlotte, North Carolina, since 1998
C&H Sugar: Crockett
Chevron: San Ramon
Clorox: Oakland
Coca-Cola Bottling: San Jose
Columbus Salami: Hayward
Cost Plus: Oakland
Del Monte: Walnut Creek
Dreyer's Grand Ice Cream: Oakland
eBay: San Jose
Fireman's Fund Insurance: Novato
Franklin-Templeton: San Mateo
Genentech: South San Francisco
Ghirardelli Chocolate: San Leandro
Hearst Corporation: New York, New York
J.C. Penney: Closed its San Francisco store in 1971
Lucasfilm: San Rafael
Netflix: Los Gatos
PayPal: San Jose

San Francisco 49ers: Santa Clara

SBC (formerly Pacific Telesis/Telephone): Acquired by AT&T; now in Dallas, Texas

Schlage Lock: Colorado

Sears: Closed its two San Francisco stores in 1975 and 1990

See's Candies: South San Francisco

Sharper Image: Farmington Hills, Michigan

Shriner's Hospital: Sacramento

Southern Pacific: Acquired by Union Pacific; now in Omaha, Nebraska

Swensen's Ice Cream: Acquired by IFC-Markham; now in Ontario, Canada

Transamerica: Purchased by Aegon Corporation; now in The Hague, Netherlands

Virgin America Airlines: Acquired by Alaska Airlines; now in Seattle, Washington

Visa: Foster City

Williams-Sonoma Catalog call center: Moved to Las Vegas, Nevada, in 1997

CHANGING BUSINESS MODELS

The mix of stores in a neighborhood shopping area can change quickly. Cell phone retailers, nail and hair salons and vape stores are all popular today, while hardware stores and shoe repair shops can sometimes be difficult to find. Certain neighborhood businesses that were taken for granted in the past simply no longer exist—fur salons for women, formalwear rental shops for men and even the simplest variety stores are mostly long gone. Sometimes, local government tries to help small business owners by attempting to control infiltration of neighborhoods by large chain stores, known as "formula retail," but sometimes those regulations work against the small independent businessperson because the overall regulatory burden today scares off all but the biggest operators.

It's sometimes difficult to remember the way San Francisco used to be. Many people worked at businesses that no longer exist or currently exist in very different forms. Whether the job involved retail, transportation, communications, financial services, education or something else, times have changed, and many businesses from yesteryear are nearly or completely gone:

American-Made Cars: In April 2011, San Francisco's last showroom selling new American-made cars—a Ford-Lincoln-Mercury dealer on Van Ness Avenue—closed its doors for the last time.

Banks: Corporate mergers, direct deposit and the proliferation of ATMs since the 1980s have all contributed to bring about a serious reduction in branch offices and staff.

Beauty Parlors: Outlets that once served large numbers of older ladies with bouffant, blue-rinsed hair have largely transitioned into unisex hair salons.

Butcher Shops: Many independent local butcher shops suffered the same fate as small neighborhood grocers when supermarkets began to take over in the 1950s.

Cigar/Smoke Shops: There were more than 150 listings for these businesses in the 1960 *San Francisco City Directory*—many located in the downtown area, but some in most neighborhood shopping areas. There are far fewer today.

Coal and Ice: Once a vital business model in every city neighborhood, stores like this are long gone.

Cocktail Lounges: Until recently, there were well over several hundred telephone directory listings for cocktail lounges, though the number has now declined, suggesting that there was a good deal of drinking going on both downtown and in residential areas in the past.

Dry Cleaners: These businesses, often run in conjunction with a laundry, have declined in number as the local workforce transitions away from formal business attire of silk dresses and wool suits in favor of more casual wear.

Fish and Seafood: Like butcher shops, these are far fewer in number today, but those now in business are excellent, including Swan's Oyster Depot on Polk Street, Sun Fat on Mission near 23rd Street and Hog Island Oyster Company in the Ferry Building.

Five-and-Ten-Cent Stores: This category covers the large chains (Woolworth, Kress, Newberry) as well as dozens of other mom-and-pop stores (often labeled "variety stores") that sold goods such as laundry and cleaning products, first-aid items, stationery and office supplies, sewing notions, penny candy and much more.

Funeral Directors: This business has drastically changed as many people now opt for simpler services or none at all. Also, even though San Francisco's population has grown since the turn of the millennium, that increase has largely been younger adults. Many older residents have shown an increased tendency to move away from San Francisco as they age, often spending their final years living near adult children in other locations.

Furriers: Until the late 1980s, when public tastes changed, dozens of furriers were located downtown and in many neighborhood shopping areas.

Gas Stations: Once prominent occupants of corner locations along busy streets (19th Avenue, Geary Boulevard, Van Ness Avenue, etc.) and in neighborhood business districts (Balboa, California, Judah, Lincoln, Noriega, Valencia, etc.) and many downtown locations adjacent to freeways, gas stations are now few and far between in some areas.

Grocery Stores: Given the hilly terrain of San Francisco, many small neighborhood grocery stores sprang up over the years to accommodate local shoppers and spare them from having to carry groceries a long distance in the days when automobiles were not a universal household amenity. Many of these establishments began disappearing with the emergence of large supermarkets in the 1950s, warehouse clubs in the 1980s and online grocery purveyors in the new millennium.

Orlando Colosimo and his brother Don at their business, Baireuther's Market, on Precita Avenue near Bernal Heights, 1949. Within the next decade, large supermarkets began replacing hundreds of small, neighborhood grocery stores throughout the City. *Scott Frischer collection.*

Packers at Sierra Candy Company on 18ᵗʰ Street in the Mission District, circa 1939. *Author's collection.*

Manufacturing: Tens of thousands of San Franciscans were once employed at businesses such as Del Monte Corporation, American Can, Hills Brothers Coffee and numerous other firms that manufactured or processed goods such as candy, paper, beer, meat, printed goods, sheet metal products and so forth. Most of this work now takes place outside San Francisco.

Movie Theatres: The post–World War II years saw the rise of television and a sharp decline in public attendance at the movies. The Noe on 24ᵗʰ Street was among the last local theatres built before the war and the first to close and be demolished (in the early 1950s). It was soon followed by the El Capitan in the Mission, the Irving in the Sunset and dozens of theatres along Market and Mission Streets, including the once-fabulous Fox. Beginning around 1980, the closures began spreading to neighborhoods across town as Alexandria, Bridge, Coliseum, Coronet, Parkside, Surf and others were shuttered.

Railroads: The San Francisco Belt Line Railroad provided service along the Embarcadero, serving shipping piers, from 1889 until 1980. Southern Pacific Railroad began managing train service on the Peninsula in 1870 and offering "high-speed" service to Los Angeles (twelve hours) in 1922. In 1971,

Amtrak took over all railroad operations in the United States, and shortly thereafter, Amtrak's main terminal was moved to the East Bay, the 3rd and Townsend station (built in 1915) was demolished and buses began providing the link to San Francisco. A new station serving only Peninsula commute service began operating at 4th and Townsend in San Francisco in 1975.

Retailers: Many large retailers have disappeared from San Francisco over the years, including City of Paris, Emporium, Livingston Brothers, I. Magnin, Joseph Magnin, Penney's, Roos-Atkins and Sears. Since the shopping habits of the public have changed, the stores that remain generally have far fewer employees than in the past.

Stationers: If San Franciscans slowed their letter-writing as postage rates climbed in the 1970s, that activity nearly came to a complete halt with the proliferation of email in the 1990s. As engraved stationery papers and preprinted business forms began to fade from the scene, most shops still in business today expanded their inventories to include a wide assortment of papers, pens, greeting cards and gift items.

Stock/Bond Transfer Agents: San Francisco was the corporate headquarters for many companies, and there were once numerous organizations dedicated to keeping track of investor ownership as recorded by stock and bond certificates. Some of these businesses handled only their own firm's accounts (Chevron, PG&E, Southern Pacific, etc.), while a number of banks, such as Bank of America (employing nearly five hundred at a South-of-Market processing center), offered their services to other firms in addition to handling their own company's stock certificates, dividend checks, annual reports and year-end accounting statements for shareholders. Since the 1990s, though, stock and bond certificates have largely been replaced with electronic "book-entry" statements, and most of the associated functions have been consolidated among organizations operating along the East Coast.

Telephone Companies: Once a hub for telecommunications, San Francisco used to be home to dozens of buildings housing switching equipment, operators and corporate offices. In addition to its flagship 140 New Montgomery headquarters, Pacific Bell had many other downtown offices—both north and south of Market Street—for its wide-ranging system, as well as numerous neighborhood "switching offices" in outlying areas. Today, with corporate offices of many telecommunications firms located elsewhere, plus changes in technology that rendered bulky equipment obsolete, telecommunications firms occupy a much smaller local footprint.

Above: Pre-1969 stock certificate for Bank of America. *Courtesy of a private collector.*

Left: Many San Franciscans still begin and end each workday on MUNI, as shown in this 1974 image. The classic West Portal Avenue facade of Twin Peaks Tunnel was demolished in 1976 for a new MUNI Metro station. *OpenSFHistory.*

Changes in the workday routine have impacted other aspects of daily life. At one time, a majority of San Francisco workers relied upon MUNI to get them to work in the downtown area each weekday morning and returned home at the end of the day. Today, while MUNI remains popular (and crowded), shifting patterns of employment as well as new modes of transportation present challenges for local planners.

Key employment centers are no longer exclusively in the downtown area. Colleges and universities around the City are now bigger destinations. Numerous San Franciscans work from home on a regular basis. Flex-time work schedules are more prevalent, causing fluctuations in ridership. BART routinely takes many San Franciscans to other cities for daily work. Alternative transportation is now utilized by large numbers of people on a regular basis, including TNCs (Transportation Network Companies) such as Uber and Lyft, plus bicycling, walking, ride-sharing and bike-sharing. Today, nearly 25 percent of San Franciscans routinely use TNCs at least once a month.

John Fabela and his wife and their fifteen children (nine girls and six boys ranging in age from three to twenty-four) attended Family Night at the Amazon Theatre on Geneva Avenue for a total price of one dollar in September 1953. *San Francisco History Center/San Francisco Public Library.*

10

ℱamily ℱun

Today, whenever there is discussion about family activities with children, the stories often involve electronics or extensive travel. Growing up in mid-twentieth-century San Francisco, family fun was decidedly lower-key, and it often varied by season.

Spring

- Children weeding the backyard while Dad mowed the lawn and Mom tended to her rosebushes was a standard rite of spring in many households. Even with a few fuchsia blossoms tossed around for fun, parents and kids managed to get a lot of work done in just an hour or so. A well-maintained backyard was a place of easy relaxation for many families. Sadly, many of these green spaces have disappeared under weeds, concrete or home expansions.
- Every year, in early spring, our family would take a ride to Fairfax to plan our summer vacation at Marin Town & Country Club. My parents would usually rent a cabin for a week or so, and Mom was adamant that we get a good one—that is, one with a standard-sized stove and refrigerator so that she did not have to deal with the tiny, apartment-sized appliances that were in some of the cabins. This was the surest sign that spring had arrived and the school year was two-thirds of the way over.

Left: A mom and daughter are shown relaxing on a sunny afternoon in the backyard of their Sunset District home on 27th Avenue, circa 1957. *Linda Moller Ruge collection.*

Below: Advertisement for a Lunar New Year event at the Chinese Culture Center, 2018. *Courtesy of a private collector.*

YEAR OF THE DOG
A LUNAR NEW YEAR ART POP-UP

OPENING 2/22 . 5-8PM
THROUGH 3/17 . 10AM -4PM

CHINESE CULTURE CENTER
750 KEARNY 3RD FL (INSIDE HILTON)
SAN FRANCISCO

- Attending the annual Chinese New Year parade was an annual treat for many families. The largest such parade outside Asia, the local event dates back to the 1860s. Many kids especially enjoyed foods that were more exotic than Mom's standard meat-and-potatoes and waiting for the dragon to pass by amid music and firecrackers.
- Once the sun began to emerge after the rainy season, Playland at the Beach became a popular destination for kids and parents from all over San Francisco. Armed with nothing more than a handful of dimes, we could while away an afternoon with carnival games, adventures in the Fun House and plenty of nutritious food, such as cotton candy, sno-cones and buttered popcorn.
- Spring cleaning around the house often wrapped up with Dad taking a trip to the dump on Junipero Serra Boulevard in Daly City. Long since filled in and developed (with a shopping center now in the dump's former location), it used to be a fascinating place with a deep

open pit, where youngsters were constantly reminded: "Don't touch anything" and "stay back from the edge."

- Opening day of Giants baseball has always been a popular draw for families. Tens of thousands of San Franciscans turned out in April 1958 to welcome the team to town.

San Franciscans welcome Willie Mays and the Giants baseball team to town with a ticker tape parade on Montgomery Street in April 1958 just prior to opening day at Seals Stadium. *OpenSFHistory*.

Advertising for St. Gabriel's annual parish picnic, 1961. *Bob Carini collection.*

- Parish picnics were a popular late spring activity in various Catholic communities, and they were often held at Marin Town & Country Club in Fairfax, Morton's Warm Springs in Kenwood or Blackberry Farm in Cupertino. Although thought to be a more recently created event, St. Cecilia Parish in the Parkside held its first annual picnic in Santa Clara County in 1918, just one year after the parish's founding.

- Many San Francisco high schools, both public and private, put on annual stage performances highlighting student talent. Audiences were filled with the younger siblings of those involved in the production, and attendance often motivated future interest in such performances. Archbishop Riordan High School had an exceptionally well-appointed facility for such productions, and their 1973 performance of *Hello, Dolly!* with director Ken Barbieri is still remembered today by appreciative audiences.

- May Day celebrations used to take place across the city—a remembrance of centuries-old European festivals marking the

Dancing around the maypole was a popular children's activity in local parks for many years. Shown here is the 1949 celebration at McCoppin Square near 22nd Avenue and Taraval Street. *OpenSFHistory.*

spring season. Dancing around a maypole, interweaving long ribbons of contrasting colors, was an exciting activity at plenty of local schools, parks and playgrounds.

Summer

- When the summer fog was especially persistent, many moms would band together and plan a short road trip (usually involving another mom with a station wagon) to the warmer climes of San Mateo County. After a leisurely drive, San Bruno or San Mateo public parks offered a free afternoon of sunshine and relaxation over a picnic lunch.
- We all knew which families had a Doughboy plastic kiddie pool in their backyards for the days of warm weather, and it was always open season at those houses when Indian summer

weather arrived. On days like that, most of the neighborhood kids could be found splashing away until the fog eventually rolled in.

- Many people liked Giants double-headers with the Los Angeles Dodgers and could be found just behind the first-base line wearing orange shirts and black baseball caps with the orange "SF" logo.

- The Ice Follies used to have a fixed run in San Francisco every summer. From June through Labor Day, the ensemble performed several shows per week at Winterland Auditorium at Post and Sutter Streets. Many dads who preferred doing something else on a Sunday afternoon dropped off moms, grandmothers and kids just before the performance with the reminder, "I'll pick you up right here when it's over."

- In 1957, a new Bay Area attraction, Santa's Village, opened in Santa Cruz County as part of a chain of themed amusement parks. Most baby boomers remember it as a fun place with swings and slides, rides, a miniature railroad, a petting zoo and a gift shop. Since Santa's Village was open year-round, the three-hour round-trip (by car) from San Francisco made it a great summer vacation activity. The attraction closed in the late 1970s.

Souvenir postcard featuring Santa's Village, circa 1960. *Author's collection.*

1980s, although by 2004, new leagues and teams were emerging.

- Many families had older relatives who lived in neighborhoods all across the City. We would often spend a Sunday afternoon visiting with them, and many of my cousins did so as well. Even today, we remember my Great-aunt Marge's numerous parakeets in her sunny breakfast room, the old-fashioned pump organ in the living room and the 1950s color television and garage-door opener that her husband, Great-uncle Bill, had assembled from a packaged kit of electronic components.
- The Children's Playground in Golden Gate Park, established in 1888 as the first public children's playground in the United States, has long been an urban oasis for family outings.
- Reading the Sunday paper was a regular activity for the whole family. Some of my favorite childhood memories involve sitting on the living room floor with Dad and reading the comics—*Blondie* and *Beetle Bailey* on the first page, then *Hi and Lois*, *Popeye* and *Ripley's Believe It or Not!* on the inside pages. My German

The Children's Playground, shown here in 1944, has undergone major renovations, most recently in 2018, as it continues to delight new generations. *OpenSFHistory.*

From the late 1920s until Labor Day weekend in 1972, the Fun House was a prime attraction of Playland at the Beach. The site's closing and demolition came quickly and with little warning. *OpenSFHistory.*

grandfather always wanted to read the *Katzenjammer Kids* with me while smoking his pipe and using an affected German accent.

- A visit to the San Francisco's Farmers Market on Alemany Boulevard was a popular weekend activity for many families. Moms were wise enough to keep their kids interested in such a visit by focusing on things like apples, strawberries, oranges and blackberries rather than only buying items such as turnips, spinach and cucumbers.

- Marathon games of Monopoly—or the newer games of LIFE, Mouse Trap, and Twister—could keep kids and adults busy on an otherwise dull afternoon.

- A night at the movies was another popular family activity. Many local theatres featured a one-price admission for the entire family. Best of all, there was a theatre in every neighborhood, so it was generally an easy walk—with no need to search for parking.

- A visit to Playland at the Beach was always a popular adventure for both kids and adults, with activities ranging from the Fun House to the diving bell, playing games of skill/chance along the midway and perhaps grabbing a bite to eat at the Hot House.

11

Dining Out

S an Francisco's proliferation of restaurants and bars is nothing new—from the time of the Gold Rush, locals have enjoyed dining out on a regular basis.

The variety of cuisines offered by local establishments reflects the ever-changing taste of customers. Downtown hofbrau restaurants once dotted the Market Street and Tenderloin areas, but as patrons became more health-conscious, brats and beer began to wane in popularity. For many decades, the "big three" cuisines—Chinese, Italian and Mexican—dominated diners' choices when dining out. Today, all that has changed.

Even before the turn of the millennium, new cuisines—especially Thai, Ethiopian, Cambodian and Vietnamese—were becoming popular. Today, it is possible to wander through even a small neighborhood shopping area like West Portal Avenue and have a world of culinary opportunities, including multiple choices for the big three cuisines and many more, including Turkish, Peruvian, Indian, Japanese, Greek and French. There are also numerous opportunities for hungry souls to enjoy burgers, pizza, deli, desserts and coffee. A wide range of options can be found in many other areas of San Francisco, offering residents a huge variety when going out to eat.

Longtime residents still have fond memories of several places that are now gone:

Bernstein's Fish Grotto: Bernstein's operated at 123 Powell Street with a distinctive ship's prow jutting forth as a facade and a nautical-themed interior. The restaurant's bar, accessible through a tiny door just to the left of the main entrance, was called the Drunken Dolphin.

Blum's: From the time before the 1906 earthquake and fire, Blum's headquarters at Polk and California Streets was the crown jewel in an empire that eventually spread across neighborhoods, downtown locations and suburban shopping malls. It was known for sweets—baked goods, ice cream, candy—and had generations of loyal followers. Sadly, the end came in the 1970s as the locations closed. Still remembered is an oft-copied coffee crunch cake.

Cadillac Bar: Opened on tiny Holland Court off Howard Street in 1982, the place was a rollicking South-of-Market lunch and after-work spot until the end of the millennium, when an expansion of the nearby Moscone

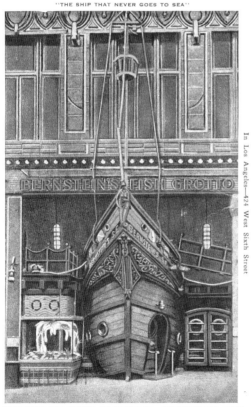

"THE SHIP THAT NEVER GOES TO SEA"

In Los Angeles—424 West Sixth Street

BERNSTEIN'S FISH GROTTO, 123 POWELL ST., SAN FRANCISCO, CALIF.

Bernstein's on Powell Street was in business from 1912 until 1981. *Glenn D. Koch collection.*

Center and development along Howard Street marked the end of bottomless margaritas, spicy food and strolling mariachis. Well into the new millennium, the scene was recreated in a new spot at 9th and Market Streets, though the atmosphere is a bit more sedate than in the lively 1980s.

Carnelian Room: Opened in 1970 atop the then-new Bank of America building at 555 California Street, the bar/restaurant with dark wood-panel elegance and a magnificent sweeping view of the City and Bay closed in December 2009 after nearly forty years in business. The space was gutted and is now leased to office tenants.

Caesar's: Opened in the mid-1950s at Bay and Powell Streets, Caesar's was a classic Italian dining establishment that provided generous portions of traditional foods in a welcoming family atmosphere. From the large serving bowls of minestrone on each table to the generous antipasto platters (Caesar's was one of the few places that routinely served pickled pigs' feet), Caesar's offerings were wide-ranging and delectable. A victim of changing tastes and neighborhood demographics, the popular spot closed in 2012 after fifty-six years of serving leisurely weekday lunches and Sunday night dinners just like Nonna used to make. As of 2019, the building remains vacant and shuttered.

Dago Mary's: Located on the grounds of the Hunters Point Naval Shipyard, the restaurant opened in 1930 as Venetian Villa, though the spot soon came to be known by the affectionate nickname that patrons gave to the manager, Mary Ghiozo. A popular place for shipyard workers, nearby residents, cops, firefighters and politicians, Dago Mary's always had a crowd digging into the generously portioned lunches and dinners. Amid the decor (acquired from Bonanza King James Flood's Atherton mansion), cocktail glasses clinked and the wine flowed among patrons, particularly during Friday lunches. Although it has been closed since 2007, the owners hope to reopen once the shipyard is repurposed, but whether this will happen remains to be seen.

Empress of China: A spectacular setting for events and wedding banquets, this popular Chinatown restaurant was in operation from 1966 to 2014 and is still missed by thousands of loyal customers.

Fosters: Fosters was a moderately priced, cafeteria-style restaurant chain that operated downtown and in many outlying areas. From morning coffee and pastries to steam-table lunch and dinner service, plus late-night meals/desserts, everyone came together and was welcome at Fosters. The chain closed in the late 1960s, though the popular English muffin brand lived on for a time.

Fosters was a cafeteria-style chain of restaurants that included twenty-four downtown and neighborhood locations from the late 1920s until 1969. This branch, at 20 Geary Street, included the standard red neon lettering against a black tile background with an eye-catching horizontal yellow stripe. Fosters locations were open from early morning hours until late at night. *San Francisco History Center/San Francisco Public Library.*

Gino's: Gino's was a longtime Financial District dining establishment owned by the Battaglieri family. Brothers Joe and Tony Battaglieri moved their family's establishment from its original location on Clay Street to Spring Street (a small, quiet alley running between California and Sacramento Streets near Kearny) in the late 1960s to make way for the construction of the Transamerica Pyramid. The new location, just across the street from Bank of America's World Headquarters building at 555 California Street, was a popular site for countless celebratory dinners in the day when corporate employees routinely marked the promotions, service anniversaries and retirements of their coworkers.

Herb's Delicatessen: Opened in 1950 by local residents Herb Thompson and his wife, Jennie, the tiny spot on Taraval Street near 32nd Avenue

Gino's

Traditionally Fine
San Francisco Cuisine!

SEVEN SPRING ST., SAN FRANCISCO • PHONE: 989-8006

Group Banquet Dinners

Salad, Antipasto, Vegetable and Potato, Dessert
and Coffee served with each Entree.

All prices include Tax and Tip.

> CHOICE IS LIMITED TO TWO ENTREES. IF MORE
> THAN TWO ENTREES ARE DESIRED — AN ADDI-
> TIONAL CHARGE WILL BE ADDED FOR THE EXTRA
> PREPARATION AND SERVICE.

ROAST CHICKEN	8.75
FILET OF SOLE	8.75
SALISBURY STEAK	8.75

BEEF STROGANOFF	9.25
BEEF BURGUNDY	9.25
POT ROAST	9.25
SHORT RIBS OF BEEF	9.25
SWISS STEAK	9.25
CHICKEN KIEV	9.25

ROAST SIRLOIN OF BEEF	9.75
LONDON BROIL	9.75
VEAL ROAST	9.75
OSSO BUCCO	9.75

VEAL PARMIGIANA	10.25
VEAL SCALOPPINE	10.25
CHICKEN GINO'S	10.25
FRIED JUMBO PRAWNS or PRAWNS MEUNIERE	10.25

ROAST PRIME RIBS OF BEEF	11.25
TOP SIRLOIN STEAK	11.25
ABALONE STEAK	11.25

NEW YORK CUT STEAK	12.75
FILET MIGNON	12.75
BROILED LOBSTER TAIL	12.75
BONELESS SQUAB stuffed with Wild Rice	12.75

Above Prices Include Tax and Tip

Gino's banquet menu from 1978, featuring generous portions, excellent service and moderate prices, all in a great downtown location with the atmosphere of a private club. *Author's collection.*

became known for hot meatball sandwiches—a recipe handed down by Jennie's Sicilian mother. Thursday was the day that an enormous stockpot of homemade meatballs could be found simmering in a hearty tomato sauce atop a vintage white porcelain gas range in the back room. Each sandwich involved one large meatball, sliced, with a splash of sauce and a choice of cheese slices served on a soft French roll and securely wrapped in layers of paper towels. In the 1980s, Herb and Jennie sold to new owner Issa Cuadra, who continued the popular neighborhood tradition for another decade. Sadly, the lease ran out in 1998 amid speculation that the building's owners wanted to construct housing. In a strange twist, the spot has remained vacant for more than twenty years.

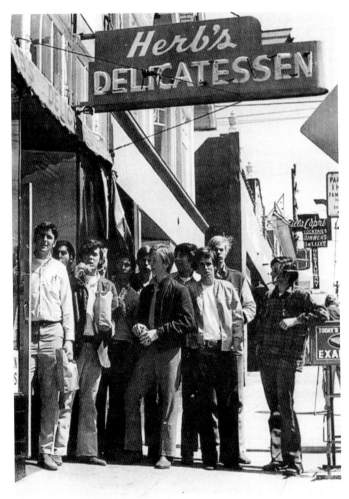

Herb's Deli on Taraval Street near 32nd Avenue became a favorite afternoon gathering spot for St. Ignatius students following the school's relocation to 37th Avenue in the fall of 1969. The young men pictured here in 1972 are now mostly retirees and grandfathers. *Kevin Carroll collection.*

Herman's: A popular longtime Richmond District deli, this spot on Geary near 7th Avenue quickly gained citywide renown. With an old-fashioned interior (including a large, highly fragrant wooden pickle barrel), Herman's carried a dazzling array of sliced meats, cheeses, salads and breads that could fulfill needs ranging from a patron who wanted a quick sandwich to catering for a lunch group. Herman's was a beloved institution until it vanished from the scene in the early 1980s. Today, there are many knockoffs of its classic San Francisco potato salad.

Hippopotamus: After taking over an old neighborhood grocery store on Van Ness Avenue in 1950, owner Jack Falvey set about creating a whimsical dining experience by hiring local artist Wolo von Trutzschler to create a motif that celebrated a smiling hippopotamus. Featuring gourmet hamburgers with sauces ranging from Béarnaise to bleu cheese to guacamole or teriyaki (and even a raw burger topped with vanilla ice cream), Hippo and its themed gift shop remained popular with young and old alike, serving families, young couples and retirees until Falvey (Lowell grad, class of '29) retired in 1987.

Lefty O'Doul's: Opened on Powell Street just after World War II, Lefty O'Doul's expanded into a popular hofbrau on Geary just west of Union Square some thirty-five years later. It closed in January 2017 following difficult lease negotiations, although a brand-new O'Doul's emerged in

Hippo Cookbook, circa 1969. *Author's collection.*

Meet "LEFTY" O'DOUL!
AT HIS BEAUTIFUL COCKTAIL ROOM
209 POWELL ST. - SAN FRANCISCO, CALIF.
A Favorite Meeting Place for Celebrities of the Sports World

ENTRANCE

The classic Lefty O'Doul's is now operating at a new Fisherman's Wharf location, where it has retained its historic collection of baseball memorabilia. *Glenn D. Koch collection.*

November 2018 at a new Fisherman's Wharf location on Jefferson Street complete with a collection of baseball memorabilia.

Leticia's: A popular 1980s dining spot on Market Street in the Castro neighborhood, Leticia's attracted long lines of diners on a nightly basis. It was known for serving generous portions of margaritas, crab enchiladas and sopaipillas (a fried pastry dessert served with honey and cinnamon and topped with vanilla ice cream). After expanding to a larger location that operated on the opposite side of the street for several years, the restaurant closed in 2011.

Lucca Ravioli Company: This small takeout deli opened at the corner of 22nd and Valencia Streets in 1925 and served the neighborhood, as well as the larger City community, until its closure in April 2019.

Pancake Palace: In the early days of San Francisco International Airport, dining options were limited—mostly quick-service or snack bar–type spots—before the arrival of Pancake Palace around 1960. Pancake Palace soon became a destination restaurant for both travelers and nontravelers. It was located in the old Main Terminal (now Terminal 2) and featured a variety of items, toppings and syrups in an atmosphere reminiscent of

Victorian San Francisco. Sadly, the place vanished in the late 1970s in a cloud of renovation dust.

Phineas T. Barnacle: In the early 1970s, the venerable old Cliff House, operating at the edge of the continent since the 1850s, began to fade as a sit-down restaurant with starched tablecloths. The place was soon subdivided into three establishments: the traditional Upstairs at the Cliff House, the more casual ground-floor Seafood & Beverage Company and a deli/bar known as Phineas T. Barnacle. All of them catered to tourists during the day, while Barnacle's attracted an evening clientele of local college students attracted by events such as ten-cent beer night. All three venues disappeared when the building was renovated and restored to the 1909 version of the Cliff House.

Portals Tavern: The quiet neighborhood bar on West Portal Avenue had been quenching thirsts for more than sixty-five years under a series of different owners until July 2019, when the building was sold and its closure announced.

Rasselas: This large Ethiopian restaurant and music venue at California and Divisadero was a popular night spot in the 1980s and 1990s, drawing appreciative crowds with both food and music. After a 1999 move to Fillmore Street's newly created Jazz District, the business continued; however, it was closed by owner Agonafer Shiferaw in 2013.

Salmagundi: This was a San Francisco–founded small chain of restaurants featuring an ever-changing array of daily soups (mulligatawny, anyone?), plus salads, sandwiches and desserts. From the early 1970s until the mid-1980s, there were Salmagundi locations throughout the downtown area serving long lines of shoppers, office workers and theatregoers. Salmagundi has been gone since the late 1980s.

The Hot House: Adjacent to Playland, this was a landmark on Great Highway from the 1930s until 1972. It relocated to Balboa Street in the Outer Richmond but has been gone since before the turn of the millennium. Loyal customers still remember the enchiladas topped with fresh raw onion and smothered in a thick, orange-hued sauce and served alongside generous quantities of sliced French bread and butter. The food may not have been authentic Mexican, but the Hot House still draws appreciative crowds when the son of the former owner hosts monthly pop-up Saturdays in an outer Richmond District location, offering sit-down and takeout service.

The Stagecoach: Located in the basement of the 1965 Wells Fargo building at the corner of Market and Montgomery Streets, this was a Financial District after-work watering hole and restaurant for decades. For the price of a

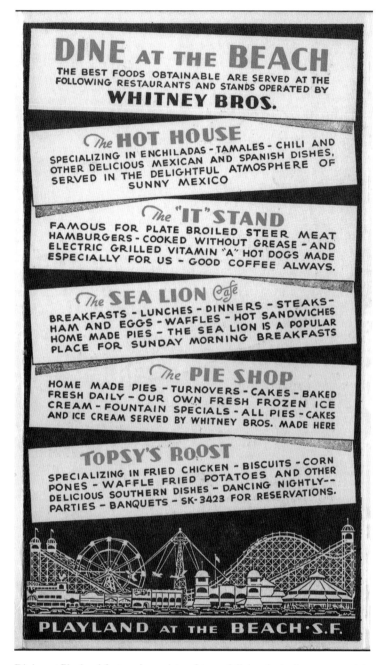

Dining at Playland featured a variety of tasty delights, including a perennial favorite, the Hot House. *Glenn D. Koch collection.*

The massive 1888 wooden structure at 3rd Street and Newcombe Avenue underwent a major renovation from 2014 to 2016 and is now known as the Bayview Opera House Ruth Williams Memorial Theatre. *Wikimedia Commons.*

acquired and renovated an imposing redbrick structure near the corner of 3rd and Mission Streets that was built as an electrical substation in 1881.

Dutch and Murphy Windmills: Constructed at the western edge of Golden Gate Park in 1907 and 1908, respectively, both mills pumped groundwater for park irrigation. After many years of being in disrepair, both mills have been restored.

Golden Fire Hydrant: Adjacent to Dolores Park is a gold-painted fire hydrant that is credited with saving the Mission District from the fires of 1906 when it somehow continued to supply water when all other nearby hydrants ran dry because of damage to underground mains.

Haas-Lilienthal House: Built in 1886, this building is the city's only intact Victorian home that is regularly open as a museum complete with period furniture and artifacts.

Holocaust Memorial: Created and installed in 1984 by sculptor George Segal, the depiction of the deceased, with a lone survivor staring out at the beauty of the Pacific Ocean, is particularly haunting. The site is owned and maintained by the San Francisco Art Commission.

Korean War Memorial: Built in 2016, the curving black marble wall—reminiscent of Washington, D.C.'s Vietnam Veterans Memorial—is located just outside San Francisco National Cemetery.

Mexican Museum: Founded in 1975 and previously housed at Fort Mason, the museum has partnered with the Smithsonian Institution to construct a new facility near 3rd and Mission Streets (due to open in 2020).

Mount Davidson Cross: Built in 1934, the 103-foot concrete cross was built through individual one-dollar donations. In 1997, in order to address concerns about a religious symbol being on public property, the site was purchased by the Council of Armenian-American Organizations as a memorial to the 1.5 million Armenians who perished during the Armenian Genocide (1915–1923).

Musée Mécanique: Originally housed at Playland (and later at the Cliff House), the museum offers free admission, though visitors must pay to use any of the more than three hundred games on display.

Museo Italo Americano: Established in 1978, the museum was the first in the United States to focus on Italian and Italian-American art and culture. Since 2008, there has been significant public outreach to acquire artifacts related to the experiences of local immigrants.

Museum of African Diaspora: Since opening in 2005, the museum has operated as a contemporary art museum celebrating Black cultures, igniting challenging conversations and inspiring learning through the global lens of the African diaspora.

Octagon House: Built in 1861, Octagon House is a San Francisco historical landmark displaying decorative arts from the Colonial and Federal periods.

Palace of Fine Arts: Originally built for the 1915 Panama-Pacific International Exhibition as a temporary structure, the palace was demolished in 1964 and replicated in permanent form. It now houses a theatre and event venue in a public park setting with a peaceful lagoon.

Portals of the Past: Once the entrance portico to the Towne Mansion on Nob Hill, the structure framed classic images of the City after the 1906 disaster. The portals were placed at the edge of Lloyd Lake in 1909, when the original site was cleared for reconstruction.

Precita Eyes: This art center supports public murals in the Mission neighborhood and was founded by Susan and Luis Cervantes in 1977.

Presidio Officers' Club: Once a social club for military officers and their families, the historic structure (with some original adobe walls) was refurbished in 2014 as the free museum and cultural center for the Presidio Trust and also houses a public restaurant and event venue.

Original Spanish fortification of the Presidio grounds, circa 1817. *Wikimedia Commons.*

Randall Museum: Founded in 1937 as the Junior Museum and operating from its current site since 1952, the facility is named for Josephine Randall, first superintendent of recreation for the San Francisco Parks Department. The museum offers free admission and features events, displays and classes mostly geared toward children.

San Francisco Fire Department Museum: The museum traces San Francisco's long history of destructive fires, highlighted with images and actual equipment dating back more than 150 years.

San Francisco Museum and Historical Society: The San Francisco Historical Society has the stated mission of preserving, interpreting and presenting San Francisco history. SFHS remains active in the community and currently has just under two thousand members.

San Francisco Museum of Modern Art: Dating back to 1935, the museum occupied space in the War Memorial Veterans Building before moving to a new location on 3rd Street in 1995. A major expansion along adjacent Mission Street was completed in 2016.

San Francisco Public Library History Center: This is a repository featuring a massive collection of books, photographs and papers related to local history.

San Francisco Railway Museum: Opened in 2006, the museum offers exhibits and archival photos of transit history and is free to the public.

SS *Jeremiah O'Brien*: This Liberty ship was built during World War II and christened for Revolutionary War captain Jeremiah O'Brien. It was part of the D-Day landing at Normandy in 1944 and was restored in time to sail to France to celebrate the fortieth anniversary of D-Day in 1984.

Tenderloin Museum: Opening its doors to the public in 2015, the museum has a mission to promote the history and character of the neighborhood by offering educational, artistic and charitable activities.

USS *San Francisco* Memorial: This 1959 memorial to one of the most decorated ships of World War II recalls the heavy damage it sustained during the Battle of Guadalcanal with a large piece of the ship's shell-riddled exterior on permanent display.

Veterans Memorial Building/War Memorial Opera House: Completed in 1932, the twin structures, designed in Beaux-Arts style, house performance space and offices of various government and arts agencies.

Virtual Museum of the City of San Francisco: Under the direction of Gladys Hansen (1925–2017), longtime historian of the San Francisco Public Library, this website continues to identify significant stories of the City and maintain them with historical accuracy.

Wells Fargo History Museum: Featuring display and interactive exhibits, this museum in the Financial District is free to the public on weekdays.

Western Neighborhoods Project: Founded in 1999 by Woody LaBounty and David Gallagher to preserve the history of western San Francisco, the group opened a public space in 2018 that hosts events, exhibits and a bookstore.

World War II West Coast Memorial: Dedicated in 1960, the memorial is a monument to lost military service members from the World War II era.

Yerba Buena Center For The Arts: Founded in 1993 as the cultural anchor of San Francisco's Yerba Buena Gardens development, YBCA's work spans the realms of contemporary art, civic engagement and public life in a rotating display environment.

13

Dearly Departed

From the earliest times of the place called Yerba Buena all the way to its growth into the City of San Francisco, locals have been departing this world on a fairly regular basis. In the early days, there were plenty of wide-open spaces dedicated as burial grounds (including more than fifty different locations), but as the city grew, most of these final resting places proved to be somewhat less than final.

When much of the early population was living in homes clustered around places like Portsmouth Plaza and the streets and alleyways South-of-Market, cemeteries emerged at the outskirts of the settled areas. A large public burial ground came to occupy land at the western stretches of Market Street near the present-day Civic Center, two Jewish cemeteries operated on the land that is now Dolores Park in the Mission District and at Lands End, beneath the Palace of the Legion of Honor, were burial grounds for many in the local Chinese community.

Space adjacent to Mission Dolores became a Catholic burial site in the late 1700s, and the grounds of the Presidio of San Francisco began accepting burials during the Spanish and Mexican eras, with the U.S. government taking over in 1846. Today, Mission Dolores and the San Francisco National Cemetery at the Presidio are San Francisco's two remaining large cemeteries.

In addition to these, a large swath of land in and adjacent to the Richmond District used to be home to four large cemeteries for more than eighty years:

Calvary: Owned and operated by the Catholic Church, Calvary opened in 1860 bounded by Geary Street, Masonic Avenue, Turk Street and St. Joseph's Avenue. In its more than seventy-five years of operation, Calvary took in more than 55,000 burials—an indicator of San Francisco's large Roman Catholic population in that era.

Laurel Hill: Opened as Lone Mountain Cemetery in 1854, this cemetery's name was changed to Laurel Hill in 1867. Fronting California Street and Presidio Avenue (and extending to Parker Avenue near Geary), the location was the prestigious final resting place for more than 35,000 San Franciscans. Among the many notable interments were cable-car inventor Andrew Hallidie, U.S. senator David Broderick and many other well-known locals, including civic and military leaders, politicians and members of socially prominent families.

Masonic: Bounded by Turk Street, Masonic and Parker Avenues and St. Ignatius Church (built in 1914) and fronting Fulton Street, this cemetery opened in 1864 and was actively managed by the fraternal order until 1901.

Odd Fellows: Originally opened in 1865 as an extension of Lone Mountain Cemetery, this cemetery—bounded by Geary Street, Turk Street, Parker Avenue and Arguello Boulevard—expanded over time and was managed by a popular fraternal organization. More than 26,000 remains were moved to Greenlawn Cemetery prior to World War II.

As early as the mid-1880s, the Catholic Church understood that its Calvary Cemetery at Geary and Masonic was no longer viable, as spaces were quickly being used up, and housing was already beginning to encroach on its south border along Turk Street. The beginnings of the current Holy Cross Catholic Cemetery had already begun in 1886, when Archbishop Patrick Riordan purchased three hundred acres of land in an area of San Mateo County that would become known as the town of Colma. Holy Cross opened for burials in 1887, though many local residents complained that it was "too far from San Francisco." Even though this cemetery has been accepting burials for more than 130 years, estimates are that with an increase in cremations (approved by the Catholic Church since 1963), Holy Cross still has sufficient space to serve the local community for the next 150 to 200 years.

There were periodic moments when there were public cries calling for the closure of the above four cemeteries. Then as now, big changes took a long time to implement. In March 1900, the Board of Supervisors passed legislation to bar new burials effective August 1, 1901. Exceptions were made in the cases of family members wishing to be buried in existing graves alongside loved ones. Calvary Cemetery, for example, took in its last burial in 1916. However, with no new sales of gravesites, the cemeteries lost their prime sources of income, as new sales had always been relied upon for the collection of perpetual maintenance fees. The Richmond District cemeteries soon fell into a state of decline.

Over the years, other local cemeteries followed the lead of the Catholic Church, and by the mid-1920s, others were acquiring land in San Mateo County. Soon, the stage was set for the mass removal of gravesites within city limits.

By the 1930s, there were renewed calls for cemeteries to be completely removed from within city limits. Lot owners in Laurel Hill objected because of the many grand monuments marking the graves of well-known wealthy San Franciscans, while the Catholic Church objected to disinterment in general out of respect for the dead who had been interred in consecrated ground.

Aerial view looking east on Geary to the Bay and Yerba Buena Island in 1938. Pictured here are Laurel Hill Cemetery (*left*), Calvary Cemetery, Lone Mountain/SF College for Women (now USF), Ewing Field (*right*), Roosevelt Junior High (now Middle) School and the San Francisco Columbarium (*near bottom*), from the former Odd Fellows Cemetery, which is now operated by the Neptune Society. *OpenSFHistory.*

The battle continued to play out at meetings of the Board of Supervisors, and by 1937, those supporting the "cemeteries must go" movement found a surprising ally in the Catholic Church, which previously had been strongly opposed.

St. Ignatius Church opened in 1914 at Fulton Street and Parker Avenue at the very edge of the Masonic Cemetery. When the adjacent college (now the University of San Francisco) began putting up its own buildings near the church in the 1920s, it became clear that the school's ability to expand was going to be severely limited by the adjacent cemetery. After negotiations between various parties, the Catholic Church officially dropped its opposition to removals but insisted upon a stricter process to be carried out at Calvary than was in place at other cemeteries. Unlike standard practices elsewhere, Archbishops William Hanna and John Mitty required that disinterment be carried out in an orderly and well-documented manner, with multiple levels of supervision and rechecking of records, plus fabric screens installed around work in progress in order to block the view of curious public onlookers. As a result, virtually no remains have surfaced at the old Calvary site (though multiple headstones have turned up), while numerous examples of overlooked remains continue to surface at other old cemetery locations.

By 1937, removals were underway at all four locations. There were numerous public notices and announcements made in the press and local churches about the timetable for removals. If bodies were not claimed and reinterred elsewhere, the city would arrange for removal and reinterment in a mass grave at one of the Colma cemeteries. Likewise, monuments had to be relocated to new sites by individual owners, and those that went unclaimed by a specified date were turned over to the Department of Public Works, which repurposed many of them as parts of the seawall at Ocean Beach or the Marina, with others being used as culverts in Buena Vista Park.

World War II then intervened, and the removal process was suspended for the duration of the war. Work resumed by 1946, and the remaining cemetery sites were quickly cleared and graded.

Removals at the Odd Fellows Cemetery commenced in the early 1930s, and workers from the WPA (Works Progress Administration) eventually built a public park and playground at the site in 1935–36, with an indoor public swimming pool added later. The imposing Columbarium, built in 1898 and part of the Odd Fellows Cemetery, is now a local landmark; it was taken over by the Neptune Society in the 1980s and refurbished, and it continues to accept new inurnments of ashes.

The land once used by the Masonic Cemetery was eventually acquired by the adjacent University of San Francisco after the bodies had been removed, and by 1950, USF had opened a new library building on the space. The campus continued expanding—with dormitories, classroom and laboratory space, a faculty residence and campus offices—from the 1950s to the present. Various construction projects over the years have unearthed multiple sets of remains from the old Masonic Cemetery.

In 1951, a new Sears, Roebuck store was built on a subdivided portion of the old Calvary site at the southeast corner of Geary and Masonic. Several decades later, that department store closed, and the building was refurbished for a number of other retailers and is now known as City Center. In 1952, Kaiser Foundation Hospital opened a new facility adjacent to the then-new Sears store and has continued to expand in that location and on adjacent properties along Geary. New housing was built in the 1950s on a series of small winding streets on the rest of the old Calvary property.

Finally, in 1953, the Fireman's Fund Insurance Company purchased the old Laurel Hill Cemetery site and constructed a new low-rise headquarters with a modern design. In the 1980s, the site was acquired from Fireman's Fund by the University of California–San Francisco, and the school's Laurel Heights campus began operating there in 1985. As the UCSF campus has completed new buildings in the Mission Bay neighborhood, a ground lease on the Laurel Heights property was negotiated with a housing developer with a provision that UCSF could temporarily remain in some of the buildings. As of 2018, plans were being put forth for more than five hundred new housing units in fifteen buildings on the site, plus one hundred thousand square feet of retail and office space, along with underground parking for nine hundred cars and six hundred bicycles.

———⟫•⟪———

Needless to say, such drastic changes in the local landscape have not always gone smoothly. News reports periodically make note of stray burial materials or human remains that have been unearthed by those working on landscaping or rebuilding projects.

Mission Dolores, San Francisco's oldest burial ground, dates to late 1782, when the site at 16th and Dolores Streets was still rural, with sheep and cattle grazing on a large portion of what is now the neighborhood. The mission, established a few blocks away in June 1776 (prior to the

Declaration of Independence), moved to its current site twelve years after it was founded. More than a century later, in the late nineteenth century, the last of approximately ten thousand burials occurred at the site, including those of Native Americans, Mexicans, Europeans and Americans. Prior to 1900, plans were underway for an extension of 16th Street to Market Street, and more than five hundred bodies were removed from the grounds—some to new locations within the remaining graveyard and about fifty to other cemeteries, including Mount Calvary, Odd Fellows and Holy Cross (in Colma). In the early 1930s, a parking lot/playground for Mission Dolores School was built over a large portion of the original cemetery grounds (which extended from Dolores Street all the way to Church Street, one block away), and while there were some removals, many other graves were left undisturbed. In the mid-1950s, a new structure for chancery offices was built at 441 Church Street atop another portion of the original cemetery grounds, with most graves left in place.

Yerba Buena Cemetery was in operation from 1850 to 1871 in the area just north of today's Civic Center (near 8th and Market Streets). When the 1880s City Hall and Hall of Records (which were damaged beyond repair in 1906 and subsequently torn down) were under construction, there were newspaper reports of stray bodies surfacing even though the area had already been cleared, with removals taken to the new City Cemetery near Lands End around 1871.

In 1908, during post-earthquake/fire reconstruction, more than twenty-five additional bodies were found. In 1934, during construction of a new federal office building at McAllister and Hyde, additional bodies were unearthed. In 2001, when the old Main Library was being retrofitted as the new Asian Art Museum, contractors found additional skeletal remains that had been buried 150 years earlier.

In 1993, the 1920s Palace of the Legion of Honor was undergoing renovations, earthquake retrofitting and a major expansion. During the course of construction work, nearly eight hundred graves were discovered beneath the museum site. These were overlooked remains from an estimated eleven thousand burials at City Cemetery, which had been established in 1870 for the interment of people who were primarily ethnic and religious minorities, as well as unclaimed bodies. Most of these interments took place prior to 1900, including some reinterments from older cemeteries in the downtown area.

By 1909, a golf course had been built on the site, and it was believed that all the bodies had been removed to Colma at the time—though the evidence now suggests otherwise. In some cases, the museum's utility lines, which date to the original construction in the early 1920s, were found to be running directly through some old caskets and even through individual skeletons.

Following the renovation work on the Legion of Honor, San Francisco officials arranged for the removal of all the found remains to Skylawn Cemetery in Colma, though it appears that many more continue to rest beneath parts of the museum that were not accessed during the reconstruction project.

⎯⎯⎯◦◦◦⎯⎯⎯

In 2016, construction workers involved in remodeling a home near Arguello Boulevard unearthed a glass-lidded casket containing a well-preserved body of a young girl beneath the home's backyard. The style of the coffin suggested that it was constructed 140 to 150 years earlier. Since the home had been built on land that was formerly the Odd Fellows Cemetery, local authorities concluded that there was no foul play involved and that the remains had inadvertently been left behind in the 1930s, when the graves were being removed. Given today's advances in science and technology, genealogists were able to research old cemetery and burial records, then digitally layered them to determine which graves were at the exact spot where the coffin was found. Further research into newspaper obituaries and other records were used to identify children buried in that part of the old cemetery. Armed with a list of possibilities, a group of volunteers then conducted additional research to trace the family trees of those who had been identified. Once this work was completed, probable descendants were located, and two of them agreed to DNA testing. The results were conclusive when one individual's DNA proved that the deceased child was his great-aunt, and that he was descended from the child's older brother. Records indicate that her name

After the removal of the Odd Fellows Cemetery, new homes and Rossi Playground were constructed in the area near Arguello Boulevard in the 1940s, with Rossi Pool added to the site in 1957. Temple Emanu-El and Roosevelt Junior High (now Middle) School are in the distance at left, and the Columbarium is at right. *OpenSFHistory.*

was Edith Howard Cook; she died on October 13, 1876, at the age of two years, twenty months and fifteen days, and she was buried in a family plot at the Odd Fellows Cemetery on October 15, 1876. She has now been reinterred at Greenlawn Cemetery in Colma.

In April 2018, excavation work in the parking lots of the old Sears store (now a retail complex known as City Center) unearthed dozens of old grave markers and monuments that had been buried since the Calvary Cemetery was redeveloped into the Anza Vista neighborhood shortly after World War II (though there were no reports of human remains being found at this location). Archaeologists were brought in to record details of the findings, and ultimately, Holy Cross Cemetery in Colma—the place where nearly forty thousand dearly departed from the old cemetery site now rest in a mass grave—accepted the material for further research and preservation.

Even though most cemeteries have been removed from San Francisco, there are still a few sites other than the National Cemetery at the Presidio, Mission Dolores Cemetery and the Columbarium in the Richmond District that contain human remains:

All Saints Episcopal: Located on Waller Street in the Haight-Ashbury neighborhood, the Chapel of the Good Shepherd houses a columbarium to honor deceased members and friends of the church.

First Unitarian Church: Pastor Thomas Starr King has been interred in the church yard facing Franklin Street since his death in 1864.

Grace Cathedral: A columbarium for the inurnment of ashes and memorial plaques was established on the second floor of the Episcopal cathedral's bell tower in 1985.

Holy Virgin Russian Orthodox Cathedral: Constructed in 1961 on Geary Boulevard in the Richmond District by pastor St. John of Shanghai and San Francisco (born Mikhail Maximovitch in 1896), the cathedral has been his final resting place since his death in July 1966.

St. Dominic's Church: In 2012, St. Dominic's Catholic Church at Bush and Steiner Streets opened 320 spaces behind the main altar, each measuring one foot square, for the inurnment of remains.

St. Gregory of Nyssa Episcopal: Founded in 1978 in the Potrero Hill neighborhood, the church maintains space for the inurnment of ashes.

St. Mary the Virgin Episcopal: Located on Union Street near Steiner, the church has 145 outdoor crypts arranged around its inner courtyard.

<hr />

Just as the landscape of cemeteries has undergone drastic change, so has the business of bidding farewell to the dearly departed. Numerous funeral directors have disappeared from the local scene in the new millennium.

With little fanfare, a multigenerational family-owned business in San Francisco closed its doors in 2017 when the funeral director firm of Valente Marini Perata closed after nearly 130 years. Originally located in North Beach, the firm—founded in 1888 by Virgil Valente, Frank Marini and John B. Perata—was a cornerstone in the Italian community. By 1926, the owners took note of the fact that many of their longtime customers had relocated to the Excelsior District during the decades after the 1906 earthquake and fire. The firm then opened a branch on outer Mission Street near Onondaga Avenue. In the 1950s, a larger, modern structure was built at the site, along with an expansive parking lot to accommodate the post–World War II shift from streetcar to automobile travel.

Even as the company's historical Italian customer base began moving to other parts of San Francisco and into the suburbs, making a telephone call to Valente Marini Perata was still the first thing that many families did after the death of a loved one. Over the years, the company also began to adapt to demographic changes by gearing its services toward the Latino and Filipino families who lived nearby, and until the very end, it remained a frequent provider of funerals and memorial services for members of local Catholic parishes, including those of St. John the Evangelist, Corpus Christi, Church of the Epiphany and Our Lady of Perpetual Help in Daly City. [Author's note: At the 1989 funeral of an old S.I./USF classmate, services began at 4840 Mission Street and then proceeded to St. Ignatius Church at Fulton Street and Parker Avenue—one of most circuitous funeral processions that most of us had ever seen. Think about it—there is simply no direct route from the Excelsior District to the northeast corner of Golden Gate Park.]

Matt Taylor, a fifth-generation member of one of the firm's founding families, let it be known in late 2016 that the Mission Street property, which was owned by his father and a partner, had been sold to a nonprofit developer with plans for 154 units of affordable housing with ground-floor retail space. A similar project was already under construction at other funeral firms, including the old Arthur J. Sullivan & Company site on upper Market Street. New housing units were also completed on 9th Avenue near Irving Street, where Hogan, Sullivan & Bianco used to operate, and Currivan's Chapel of the Sunset on Irving Street had become an office building decades earlier.

Valente Marini Perata was exploring relocation options for the firm, including the possibility of an onsite operation at the Italian Cemetery in Colma, but sadly, those plans did not come to pass. One of the last funerals held at Valente's Mission Street location was in July 2017 for a longtime resident who was nearly ninety-six years old and a graduate of nearby Balboa High School and Cogswell College (when it was located at 26th and Folsom Streets) and had spent a lengthy career working for the federal government. Not surprisingly, that last service included a traditional wake for the deceased from 5:00 to 9:00 p.m. on one day, followed by her funeral Mass at nearby Corpus Christi Church on Santa Rosa Avenue and Alemany Boulevard the next morning. This is the way things were conducted for decades at Valente Marini Perata and elsewhere, but in recent times, mourning customs in San Francisco have significantly changed.

Several factors have impacted the local funeral industry, including:

- Fewer people dying in San Francisco (9,658 deaths in 1970 vs. 6,008 in 2015, even though the city's population increased by 150,000 in that time frame).

- Fewer deaths of middle-aged people in the workforce (primarily due to better health care and practices). Services for younger individuals generally attracted larger numbers of extended family, friends and coworkers, most of whom were living in the area.
- Fewer traditional funerals with open caskets and multiday visitation, along with an increase in the number of less-costly cremations with abbreviated services and private scattering of ashes—and sometimes no services at all.

Among Catholics, cremation was once forbidden, but it has been accepted by church law since 1963, and its use has significantly expanded since then—even among firm adherents. Likewise, there has been a greater acceptance of cremation among many observant Jewish families. Sinai Memorial Chapel, the traditional Jewish funeral director in San Francisco, notes on the firm's website that it is able to accommodate a family's wishes for cremation and a memorial service as an alternative to that faith's traditional practice, which specifies in-ground burial in a plain wooden casket within twenty-four hours of death.

San Francisco was once dotted with funeral establishments, which often marketed their services to specific ethnic groups or neighborhood districts. From the 1920s through the 1950s, there were more than fifty listings for such businesses in each annual edition of the *City Directory*. By 1960, the number had dropped to forty-two, and by 1973, the count was down to thirty-seven. Today, that number has dwindled to just twelve.

Clearly, it is rare that a family business manages to thrive for three full generations while still making meaningful contributions to the community. Sometimes, a company will fail to keep pace with changing times (for examples, think of buggy-whip manufacturers, telephone answering services or typewriter repair shops), while in other cases, operations may be moved to another country for the purposes of reducing taxes and/or production costs (such as manufacturers of everything from clothing to food products to automobiles).

Arthur J. Sullivan & Company, a family-owned/operated firm in business for more than ninety years quietly serving the needs of the community, left its longtime location on upper Market Street in 2016. The firm had merged with Duggan's Serra Mortuary in Daly City several years earlier, and Sullivan's Market Street site was slated to be replaced by a condo-retail complex.

Readers should not blame this particular change on changing times involving technology takeovers or unscrupulous landlords. The next generation of Sullivans—brothers Arthur III and Jim—were both well past the usual age for retirement, and the younger generations of the family already had other careers and were not interested in taking over daily management duties.

The business began in the years just after the end of World War I, when Arthur J. Sullivan (the first), who lived with his family near the southeast corner of Golden Gate Park, went into business with his brother Alfred at 2254 Market Street, with the sign reading "Arthur J. Sullivan, Undertakers." Over time, Arthur Jr. (the son) took over the business, and the sign was changed to include the industry's then-standard moniker: "Funeral Directors."

In the early twentieth century, death was, sadly, a frequent visitor in most households. The lack of antibiotics, plus limited diagnostic testing/preventative medical treatments, took many San Franciscans to early graves. Childbirth was the largest single cause of death among otherwise healthy young women. Today, most who die at younger than age ninety are said to have "gone too soon"—only the AIDS epidemic that began in the 1980s bears a similarity to the earlier era when funerals frequently involved younger people who were often in the prime of their lives.

San Francisco was dotted with funeral establishments in the 1920s, with more than fifty listings in each annual edition of the *City Directory*. Services were just beginning to be held outside the home, and various establishments were striving to provide a homey atmosphere for prefuneral visitation and for the service itself (if the family was not planning to have a church service).

This was also a time when the automobile was a comparative rarity in many households, so undertaking parlors tended to be conveniently located in virtually every San Francisco neighborhood in order to provide easy access for mourners. In the 1920s, many firms had horse-drawn hearses, and the public transit system even offered electric streetcars specifically for funerals; these ran to the Colma cemeteries via Mission Street and the center median of El Camino Real. Firms like Sullivan's were among the first to introduce that new amenity—the automobile—for transporting both the casket and the mourners.

This was a business model that used to maintain a regular clientele, with families returning again and again to the same firm during times of need. Jewish families generally sought the services of Sinai Memorial Chapel, while most Italian families gravitated to Valente Marini Perata. The once-large San Francisco Irish community had split loyalties, with many favoring

Street scene showing funeral director Arthur J. Sullivan & Company, at 2254 Market Street, circa 2002. *David Seibold image.*

Carew & English, located for years at Masonic and Golden Gate Avenues. The Mission District was home to several establishments—Duggan's, Driscoll's, Reilly Company/Goodwin & Scannell—while the Richmond District had McAvoy & O'Hara at 10th Avenue and Geary Boulevard, plus Ashley & McMullen at 6th Avenue. Sunset District residents might have selected Hogan & Sullivan on 9th Avenue or Currivan's Chapel of the Sunset on Irving Street. Carew & English and Arthur J. Sullivan were used by many people across the entire city.

Gradually, consolidations began to occur, and numerous firms vanished. Some of those still in business, such as Halsted & Co. on Sutter Street, are an amalgam of many different firms with deep roots in San Francisco history. A sign at Halsted indicates that their firm has absorbed N. Gray (a Gold Rush–era coffin-maker that survived well into the twentieth century), Carew & English, Gantner-Felder-Kenny (previously at Market and Duboce Streets), Gantner-Maison-Domergue, H.F. Suhr Company, Godeau Funeral Home, Martin & Brown Funeral Directors and Quock Fook Sang Mortuary. Some of the Halsted records go back to N. Gray's services, with transactions dating to the 1850s.

Even into the 1950s and 1960s, funerals were often enormous events, because many individuals died at relatively young ages, in their working years and with many friends and relatives still living in San Francisco. Sullivan's experienced congestion in their small parking lot in those days, and the family member in charge at the time, Arthur J. Sullivan Jr., a lifelong Sunset District resident, purchased a dilapidated old structure facing 16th Street, had it demolished and created a larger lot to accommodate the constant stream of cars bringing mourners to the establishment each day and night for visitations.

During the onset of the AIDS epidemic in the early 1980s, Sullivan's was recognized by the San Francisco Department of Health as being one of the only funeral establishments that would provide services to AIDS victims. The Sullivan family was long known for possessing generous quantities of both common sense and compassion.

In 1986, Arthur Jr. passed away, and his wife, Catherine, took over the business, overseeing the work of her two sons, Arthur III and Jim (with one living in the Parkside and the other near West Portal). The business changed with the times, as the brothers noted that more and more local residents were opting for simpler funerals, often with cremation instead of open-casket viewing. Changing migration patterns, particularly among their largely Irish-Catholic clientele, meant that many families who once availed themselves of Sullivan's services were no longer residing in the area. In 2009, Sullivan's completed a merger agreement with Duggan's Serra Mortuary, another firm with deep roots in the San Francisco community, setting the groundwork for the 2016 transition.

It's interesting to note that within the western neighborhoods of San Francisco, many mothers of baby boomers used to share a wry expression among themselves that defined their personal wishes for aging in place as they grew older. Dozens and dozens of them (this writer's own mother included), mostly widows, regularly announced to family and friends that "the only person who will ever get me out of my house is the undertaker—and that will be feet-first." We boomers generally tried to abide by such strongly held wishes.

The Duggan family, with its younger generations still moving into management positions within their family-owned firm, took over completely in 2016. The Market Street building is slated to become retail space, while the large adjacent parking area will be the home of new housing units.

I'll likely wander through that new space whenever some future retailer sets up shop just for a final look at the spot where my own family once said goodbye to so many loved ones.

Natives will also point out that many undertakers were conveniently located so as to be just steps away from a friendly neighborhood watering hole—many of which have also disappeared based on reduced attendance following the closure of a nearby funeral establishment. Sometimes, mourners took it upon themselves to give the dearly departed a proper send-off right there on the premises of the funeral home. One of this author's high school classmates reported that his grandfather's 1961 wake at Carew & English on Masonic Avenue was such a boisterous affair (friends of the deceased had a full bar operating out of the men's room, with cases of whiskey, boxes of cocktail glasses and hundred-pound sacks of ice—with some mourners dancing in the lobby) that his family was banned from that particular establishment in perpetuity!

Florists, too, have experienced drastic changes in their businesses because of shifting mourning patterns. Newcomers have sometimes commented about the number of florist establishments around 16th and Mission Streets. Old-timers continue to remind them that many local funeral directors were once located on Mission or Valencia Streets, and the No. 40 streetcar line to San Mateo County once ran directly through that intersection before heading down El Camino Real/Mission Road to "cemetery row"—although that interurban line was eliminated in 1948–49.

The Parkside District's St. Cecilia Church has been the scene of thousands of funerals and memorial services since it was completed in 1956. The parish celebrated the 100th anniversary of its founding in 2017. *Mary Ellen (MER) Ring.*

In the past, friends and relatives might send a floral wreath, a standing spray, a live plant or a basket of flowers to the funeral home in time for the traditional after-work visitation hours and/or the next day's before-church services. As late as the 1970s, it was not at all unusual to see dozens of floral pieces on display at an average funeral, although today, such tributes are often limited to those from the immediate family.

Even printed newspaper obituaries—once widely referred to as "the Irish Sporting Green" by many faithful daily readers—are considerably shorter in length and fewer in number in recent times, with the cost of even brief notices often exceeding several hundred dollars. These days, many death announcements mention "donations to your favorite charity preferred," while San Francisco newspapers have historically been reluctant to offend the floral industry and generally avoided using the stark phrase: "No flowers."

Little by little, even death is undergoing significant changes as more and more of the daily rituals from our collective past slowly fade from the scene.

14

Getting around Town

O ther than major earthquakes and widespread conflagrations, some of the most dramatic alterations to the San Francisco landscape have occurred when changes in transportation methods were introduced into the local landscape.

Surely, there were complaints in the nineteenth century as sand dunes along Market Street were being cleared to allow for installation of tracks for new streetcars that were pulled by horses that regularly "polluted" the area. As mechanical cable cars and electric-powered traction replaced horse cars, there were concerns over noise. As streetcar lines expanded into outlying areas, locals were often upset over the cost of extending such services to sparsely populated neighborhoods, even though such expansions invariably paid off in the long run.

By the 1930s, the automobile had come into its own. At a point far out in the sand dunes, Sunset Boulevard was constructed as a tree-lined north–south thoroughfare running between 36th and 37th Avenues. Several years later, many homes and businesses along the stretch of 19th Avenue south of Golden Gate Park were moved to accommodate the widening of the street to three lanes in each direction for the increasing flow of traffic to and from the Golden Gate Bridge, and Lombard Street in the Marina was given a similar makeover for the same reason.

By the 1940s, the automobile began to intrude even further into the lives of many local residents as new streets, freeways and parking facilities were built to accommodate the daily flow of traffic. Older buildings,

Sutro Terminal, just a few steps uphill from Sutro Baths and the Cliff House, circa 1928. The wooden station was built in the late 1890s. Passengers could ride a streetcar direct from downtown and wait for the return trip in a weather-protected area complete with refreshment stands. The cavernous structure burned in a spectacular fire in February 1949 and was never rebuilt, as the streetcars were set to be replaced with buses. *OpenSFHistory.*

The wide-open expanses of land adjacent to Sunset Boulevard, shown here looking north from the Sloat Boulevard overpass in 1932, have long since disappeared under a blanket of homes and businesses. *OpenSFHistory.*

including commercial and residential units, were demolished in the downtown area as dozens of new parking lots and garages were built to absorb all those vehicles.

One-way streets and parking meters were introduced to San Francisco prior to World War II. These changes helped to keep traffic moving, though they have caused some degree of consternation to many drivers over the years.

The underground, four-level Union Square Garage, built at the outset of World War II, was among the first of many City-built parking facilities in the downtown area. It was soon followed by Downtown Center Garage at Mason and O'Farrell Streets, Ellis-O'Farrell Garage, Fifth & Mission Garage, Sutter-Stockton Garage and many more. By the late 1960s, even the beloved old White House (a department store that had gone out of business

X-1758 - 7/13/48 MUNI.RY. GEARY ST. WIDENING *VIEW E, TOWARD GEARY ST.& PRESIDIO AVE,*

Post–World War II street-widening and streetcar track project on Geary near Masonic Avenue, 1948. The former site of Calvary Cemetery (open from 1860 to 1940) in the background has been cleared and would soon be filled with homes and businesses, including a new Sears store. Streetcar lines crisscrossed every neighborhood and were an important link at a time when many people did not own an automobile. *San Francisco Metropolitan Transportation Agency (SFMTA) Photo Department and Archives.*

Streetcar from the old No. 17 line crossing Ulloa Street in 1940 toward the terminus at Wawona, with Larsen Park at right. This line's route explains why 20th Avenue in the Sunset District is wider than standard north–south avenues. *OpenSFHistory.*

As San Francisco becomes increasingly modern, it is hard to imagine that horses were still a small part of the transportation picture in this image from the corner of Laguna and McAllister Streets in the 1940s, with some "pollution" clearly visible in the foreground. All the McAllister Street buildings shown at left were demolished as part of urban renewal in the 1960s and 1970s. *OpenSFHistory.*

Downtown Center Garage at the time of completion in 1953. *Author's collection.*

in 1965) had its interior gutted and a parking structure constructed within its venerable exterior walls.

Today, parking meters operate on "variable demand pricing"—an electronic system that automatically adjusts rates based on the day of the week, time of day and demand for parking in a particular area. Parking for two hours on a Friday night near a popular neighborhood dining spot will cost considerably more than a visit to an adjacent business on a quiet Tuesday morning. The program, which started testing in 2008, was expanded to include all local parking meters in 2018. Today, the City's twenty-eight thousand meters accept coins, credit cards, pay-by-phone and prepaid cards. Meters now operate every day of the year except Thanksgiving, Christmas and New Year's Day, with rates ranging from fifty cents per hour (in many locations) to seven dollars per hour (near the Giants ballpark during game times). "Saving pennies for the meter" is no longer practical, as the one-cent coins have not been accepted by meters for many years.

In spite of some well-publicized meltdowns and occasional glitches, MUNI operations are vital to San Francisco. The system now operates fifty-four bus lines, seventeen trolley bus lines, seven streetcar lines, three cable car lines, and two heritage streetcar lines serving well over two million riders per year.

And then, there are the freeways.

By 1948, the San Francisco Planning Department was envisioning a network of freeways crisscrossing the entire city. These ideas changed slightly in 1951 (and again in 1955) and became known as the Trafficways Plan. One of the primary features in the drawings was something known as the Western Freeway, a north–south link from the area near San Francisco International Airport (which had undergone a massive expansion with a

West Portal Avenue stop for K-L-M streetcar lines emerging from the Twin Peaks Tunnel, 1965. *OpenSFHistory.*

new terminal in 1954) that traveled in a virtual straight line to the Golden Gate Bridge. Fortunately, neighborhood opposition quickly formed, and the plan was scuttled, though not before many residents, fearful that their homes might be gobbled up for a new freeway, opted to leave San Francisco for new homes in the suburbs.

There was still some lingering political support for freeways, and in 1959, the Embarcadero Freeway began to take shape, snaking along the city's waterfront. As more homes and businesses were moved or demolished to create space for US 101 south from Bayshore Boulevard to San Mateo County, plus Interstate 280 near the old Alemany Boulevard right-of-way, a full-scale "Freeway Revolt" took place in San Francisco, with politicians finally beginning to understand the public's deep-seated opposition.

Another major upheaval in the local landscape occurred in November 1962, when voters in San Francisco, Alameda and Contra Costa Counties approved a sales-tax increase that led to the construction of BART (Bay Area Rapid Transit). Due to a then-recent change by the state legislature, the approval requirement for such measures had just been lowered from a two-thirds majority (66 percent) to a more achievable 60 percent. The measure passed by a thin margin (61.2 percent) to become the largest single public works project ever undertaken in the United States by local citizens.

Intersection of Milton Street and Cayuga Avenue, circa 1960. Homes were being cleared to make way for a freeway that would become known as Interstate 280. Scenes like this helped solidify public opposition to further freeway construction in San Francisco. *OpenSFHistory.*

BART construction and its eventual operations have changed many aspects of daily life in and around San Francisco.

The project's kickoff in San Francisco began in July 1967, when digging began for the tunnels and stations beneath San Francisco's Market Street. No one who lived or worked in the city at the time will ever forget the noise, dirt and disruptions caused by the massive project. It has been estimated that at the height of construction, in 1969, there were more than five thousand workers on the job every business day. By 1971, the subway tunnel was "holed through" at the west end of the Montgomery Street station.

BART began regular service between the downtown Oakland and Fremont stations in the East Bay in September 1972 before expanding when other lines were completed. Service from downtown San Francisco to Daly City commenced in November 1973, and full service through the Transbay Tube finally began in September 1974. Suddenly, new housing developments in the East Bay became easily accessible to many San Francisco residents, and at a low cost, opening up many new possibilities.

Over the years, BART has improved service throughout the system, including an infill Embarcadero station added in downtown San Francisco in 1976, a new line to San Francisco International Airport that opened

In 1967, nearly five years after voters approved an increase in sales tax to pay for BART, dozens of local schoolchildren helped kick off one of the largest construction projects in San Francisco history—the BART/MUNI subway. Note the commemorative ribbons reading, "DIG IN, DIG IN. Market Street Subway, July 25, 1967." Many of these youngsters are now old enough to collect Social Security. *San Francisco Metropolitan Transportation Agency (SFMTA) Photo Department and Archives.*

in June 2003 and several new East Bay extensions, with work currently underway to extend the system into parts of Santa Clara County. More sophisticated computer systems now allow better headway between trains than in the early days, though the system's current increased ridership is clearly straining capacity.

Meanwhile, MUNI's new tunnel for streetcars, which was under construction in the downtown area concurrently with the building of BART, continued west to Duboce Avenue, where the J–Church and N–Judah lines

Nearly eleven years to the day from when voters approved funding for BART and after more than six full years of a disruptive construction zone all along Market Street, passengers display nonchalant looks on the first day of BART service in San Francisco. This picture was taken aboard a train at the Powell Street station on November 3, 1973. *San Francisco Metropolitan Transportation Agency (SFMTA) Photo Department and Archives.*

would eventually exit the subway. Further tunneling then continued to Castro Street, where the K–L–M lines would eventually enter the 1917 Twin Peaks Tunnel seamlessly from the subway. Although subway construction was completed in 1978, it was not until February 1980 that MUNI Metro operations commenced weekday revenue service in the subway, first with the N–Judah line, then other lines and hours being gradually added. In November 1982, full MUNI Metro service finally began operating seven days a week.

During the course of MUNI Metro construction, Market Street access to the existing Twin Peaks Tunnel sometimes required elaborate streetcar detours at Castro Street, shown here in 1973. *San Francisco Metropolitan Transportation Agency (SFMTA) Photo Department and Archives.*

In 1982, to compensate for a planned shutdown of cable car lines for a massive two-year overhaul, MUNI began running historic streetcars on Market Street. The line was designated "F-Market & Wharves" and was so popular that it was continued until 1987. In 1995, the line was permanently established, replacing the No. 8–Market trolley bus route.

In 1980 and 1991, respectively, the M–Oceanview and J–Church streetcar lines were extended to Balboa Park as a link to BART. In 1998, the N–Judah line's terminus was extended from the Embarcadero station to the site of the new ballpark South-of-Market. In 2001, MUNI inaugurated service on a new S–Shuttle line running from Castro Station to stops at the Caltrain station and baseball stadium. In 2007, the new T–3rd Street line commenced, running from Castro through the MUNI Metro subway and then exiting the subway just beyond the Embarcadero station to run south to Bayshore Boulevard and Sunnydale Avenue. In 2015, MUNI established the E–Embarcadero heritage streetcar line with service to the Fisherman's Wharf area.

In 2019, construction is nearing completion on the Central Subway, with planned at-grade and subway service on the T-line from its southern terminus at Bayshore Boulevard to Chinatown station, with intermediate stops at Caltrain, Moscone Center and Union Square (beneath and connected to the BART/MUNI Metro subway). Other major projects under consideration include undergrounding a portion of the M–Oceanview line between West Portal station and the stops serving Stonestown and SFSU/ Parkmerced, plus dedicated bus rapid transit lanes along both Van Ness Avenue and Geary Boulevard.

In the summer of 2018, a new transit terminal opened to replace the 1930s East Bay Terminal. Now known as Salesforce Transit Center (for the adjacent office tower, which is now San Francisco's tallest building), the multistory building, with four stories above the street and two subterranean levels, is located just south of Mission Street between Second and Beale Streets. The first phase of the project opened with bus service from the East Bay, Greyhound and Amtrak Thruway bus service connecting with MUNI lines. The center is also the terminus for multiple MUNI lines, including the 5–Fulton, 7–Haight/Noriega, 14–Mission, 25–Treasure Island and 38– Geary. Phase Two will see the terminal as the new San Francisco destination for Caltrain service from the Peninsula, and eventually, California High Speed Rail trains from Southern California will travel into an underground station

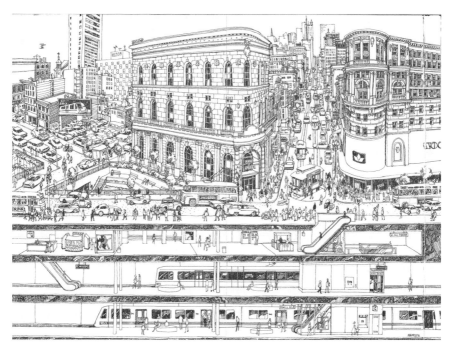

Old advertisement depicting the ever-lively intersection of Market and Powell Streets with a diagram of the then-new Market Street subway, circa 1973. Hallidie Plaza and 1 Powell Street are at left, with the Woolworth store and Flood Building at right. Today, there are many more hotel buildings in this area. *Author's collection.*

with links to other transit routes on upper levels. The building also includes a rooftop public park, retail space, bicycle parking and administrative offices.

There has been recent discussion about the need for upgrades to BART's aging infrastructure and the possibility of a second Transbay Tube to accommodate increased train frequencies. This has led to the possibility of a new BART line extending from downtown west beneath Geary Boulevard to the vicinity of USF, then turning south with a tunnel beneath 19th Avenue (with theoretical stations at Judah, Taraval and Stonestown/SFSU) before rejoining the main BART line at Daly City.

Whatever the future holds, it is certain that San Franciscans will always be seeking newer and better ways of getting around town.

15

Lazy, Hazy, Crazy Days of Summer

S an Francisco kids have always known that each school year is marked at its beginning and end by oppressively hot weather. In fact, the hottest days in San Francisco have invariably occurred in June or September. During summer vacations, though, much of the city is surrounded by a cool, swirling mist of fog. "Clearing to near the coast by dusk" is a dismal but regular summertime weather report for several neighborhoods.

What are school kids to do for entertainment under those circumstances? Unlike today's electronics-addicted youth, in the past, we all had plenty of low-tech options to amuse us—even in the summer fog.

Art: Many parents wisely kept a supply of old newspapers, Play-Doh, finger paint, colored chalk, papier-mâché and various other supplies to occupy kids when school was not in session.

Board Games: Most homes had a few standard boxed games tucked away in the front hall closet, including checkers, chess, Monopoly, Password, Scrabble, Skunk and Yahtzee, plus a deck of playing cards and a collection of poker chips. Some of my cousins had a very wise mother who regularly told us, "If you can sing, dance, and play cards, you will always be able to have fun."

Camp: Whether it involved daytime activities at Silver Tree in Glen Canyon or sleepovers in places ranging from CYO Camp in Occidental to Camp Ben Swig in Saratoga, camp was usually a love-it-or-hate-it experience for

Children holding flags from Silver Tree Camp, circa 1950. The City-run day camp in Glen Canyon Park now serves two hundred children per week from June until August and has been in operation since 1941. *OpenSFHistory.*

most youngsters. In the past, the focus was roughing it in the great outdoors, but today, summer camps usually have a specific theme, including designing comics, painting, computer programming, language immersion, math, cooking, science, nature, photography or architecture.

Collecting: Empty cigar boxes from the corner drugstore were not just for school supplies. During the summer, these free handouts contained various collections of coins, stamps, bottlecaps, rocks, seashells, baseball cards or whatever else struck a child's interest. Coin-collecting often took the form of walking from bank to bank along a couple of flat blocks of a neighborhood commercial corridor (Clement, Irving, West Portal) and buying a fifty-cent roll of pennies, then sorting through them for desired dates/mint marks, replacing the ones that were selected and rerolling them in fresh wrappers and exchanging for a new roll at the next bank down the street. Just for the record, I'm still looking for that ever-elusive 1909-S (for San Francisco) Lincoln penny.

Disneyland: Visiting here was every kid's summer wish. Prior to the 1970s, most families handled this as a road trip with frequent snack/restroom breaks before spending the night somewhere along the coast near Santa Barbara. Also included in the itinerary would be a visit to Marineland of the Pacific—an aquarium/amusement park that operated from 1954 to 1987 on the Palo Verde peninsula of Los Angeles County. Each family's long-anticipated arrival at Disneyland via the Harbor Freeway was marked by excited screams of "we're here!" as vehicles slowly crept toward their final destination. Primed by schoolmates and Disney's Sunday night TV program, everyone knew which attractions they wanted to visit first and which were the scariest—although prior to the 1980s, only the Matterhorn bobsleds could truly be described as a "thrill ride." No visit to Orange County was complete without a chicken dinner (including biscuits served with legendary boysenberry jam) at the nearby Knott's Berry Farm. Throughout the entire vacation, kids ingested tons of waffles and gallons of maple syrup for breakfast each day, plus dozens of hot dogs for lunch, while accumulating endless happy stories to share with classmates in September.

Fireworks: Fireworks have long been banned in San Francisco, but in the 1950s and '60s, we invariably made the trek to the parking lot of the Westlake Shopping Center to purchase all sorts of materials with which to celebrate our nation's independence. When the big night came, virtually every block in the Sunset and Richmond Districts was filled with children and teenagers—all dressed in heavy jackets to ward off the fog—setting off a variety of pyrotechnics. As we got older, we began to hear that even more spectacular devices were readily available on the streets of Chinatown. Many kids from the western neighborhoods quickly learned that taking a MUNI streetcar down Market Street and transferring to the 30–Stockton bus would have them shopping on Grant Avenue in about half an hour. By the late 1960s, sedate sparklers were replaced by cherry bombs and bottle rockets that made the entire city feel like it was under siege. Neighbors, especially the notoriously cranky ones—"You kids stay off my lawn!"—were constantly on their toes for weeks before and after the holiday as random firecrackers were set off in the tunnel entrances of their homes.

Giants Baseball: Afternoon games at Candlestick Park usually had a fair chance of sunny weather, even during a San Francisco summer. Saturday double-headers were a special bargain, with a one-dollar general admission ticket until at least the late 1970s. MUNI helped increase attendance numbers considerably by running a special line—the Ballpark Express—along major streets such as Geary Boulevard, Van Ness Avenue and 19th Avenue, so direct travel to Candlestick was fast, cheap and easy, often requiring no transfers.

Willie McCovey and youthful fans at Candlestick Park, summer of 1961. *OpenSFHistory.*

Golden Gate Park: The ultimate kids' recreation spot, easily accessible by walking, biking or taking MUNI. In bygone days, admission to the museum, aquarium and planetarium was free, though today, there is still one free day per month for local residents.

Helping Out: Every family seemed to have an elderly relative who needed some assistance. Many kids were assigned to grandparent patrol one or two days each month—mowing/watering lawns, trimming shrubs, cleaning out basements or helping with daily chores around the house. Some earned a bit of extra spending money doing things like this, with the added benefit that most grandparents would provide unlimited treats with a conspiratorial warning: "Don't tell your parents."

Ice Skating: Thousands remember the 48th Avenue ice rink at Sutro's, as well as two owned by Ice Follies stars Phyllis and Harris Legg (one on Ocean Avenue and another at 11th and Market Streets). Sutro's continued to offer ice skating until its final closure in 1966 and subsequent fire, though swimming had been discontinued by January 1954 due to maintenance issues.

Library Visits: Local public libraries represented a peaceful oasis from squabbling siblings, blaring TVs and parents who decided it was high time that you cleaned your room. In those days, libraries emphasized reading and research (rather than after-school day care)—though there was a certain social atmosphere in the evenings, when teenagers congregated in order to "run into" members of the opposite sex until the 9:00 p.m. closing time.

Marin Town & Country Club: Even today, nearly fifty years after this Fairfax recreation spot was permanently closed, the name still evokes warm nostalgia among those who visited it—particularly during the peak years of the 1950s and 1960s.

Movies: In the 1960s, kids had the freedom to bike, walk or take MUNI virtually anywhere in San Francisco. Neighborhood movie theaters were great places to socialize with friends, even when the film was not so good. The Parkside Theater offered a terrific bargain in the summer of 1962—matinees on Tuesdays and Fridays for just twenty-five cents (or one dollar and thirty cents for a thirteen-event season ticket). For just a handful of coins, thousands of kids were entertained and fed for an afternoon, as older youth earned the minimum wage (then about one dollar per hour) while aiming flashlights and whispering "Shhhhh!" to sugar-crazed mobs of youngsters. Many can still see the popcorn raining down at regular intervals from the balcony of the Parkside onto the heads of patrons in the floor seats. Seats at the back of the main floor were highly prized as being "safe" from such incidents and filled up quickly.

My Summer Reader: This weekly newsmagazine for kids continued the theme of *My Weekly Reader* (distributed during the school year) with age-appropriate articles, games, puzzles and comics. Many youngsters felt quite grown up receiving weekly mail addressed with their names.

Playland: Armed with a handful of coins and a student "car ticket" for MUNI, most 1960s kids could amuse themselves and also fill up on a variety of unhealthful snacks along the midway that local government would likely ban today. The Fun House offered the best bargain in the place. For a mere ten cents in the late 1950s (or seventy-five cents by the early 1970s), visitors could explore for hours, going from the rotating padded entrance gates and mirrored maze to the cavernous interior, where female visitors had to have been concerned that an unseen operator controlled blasts of air from the floor that would lift a skirt. Venturing deeper into the old wooden building on walkways and stairs that flexed up and down, there was the Joy Wheel, the rotating barrel, rocking horses, an incredible multistory polished-wood slide that ran from high in the rafters to the main floor and much more. By the late 1960s, many parents felt that it was no longer safe to allow younger children to visit Playland unsupervised. Business declined, and the beloved spot closed on Labor Day weekend in 1972. It was promptly demolished and eventually replaced by nondescript condos.

Roller Skating: When Playland adventures were completed, kids could also visit Skateland, an adjacent indoor roller rink at Great Highway and Balboa Street.

Russian River: Whether one's destination was Guerneville, Monte Rio or Rio Nido, Sonoma County has been a summer getaway for generations of San Franciscans going back to the late nineteenth century. Once accessible mainly by train, after World War II, road improvements made the area easily reachable from the City by car in just over an hour.

San Mateo Park: In the early 1950s, many housebound moms, cooped up during cold foggy spells, would experience symptoms of "cabin fever" by midsummer. A couple of them would band together with a mom who owned a station wagon and haul a group of youngsters to the sunshine in San Mateo's Central Park along El Camino Real. With spacious picnic grounds, swings, slides, a baseball diamond and even a miniature train circling the park, it gave many San Franciscans a much-needed dose of summer sunshine.

Scouts: Scouting offered a variety of summer programs for members, including sports, crafts and field trips.

A clothing label from the 1960s. The Bruce Bary store in Stonestown Mall was a popular shop that carried classic prep clothing for boys and young men from the 1950s until the 1970s. *Author's collection.*

Shopping for School Clothes: Whether they headed to City of Paris or Sue Mills for Catholic school uniforms, Stonestown's Bruce Bary for prep wear or the aisles of Emporium, Sears, J.C. Penney or GETs, by mid-August, everyone was out shopping for back-to-school clothing.

Stern Grove Concerts: The free summer concert series, which began in 1938, offer a great summertime activity for everyone.

Summer Reading: In the past, many schools, both public and private, assigned summer reading lists to their students. Despite constant protests (deemed "whining" by parents), this practice helped many of us expand our literary skills while also offering parents some much-needed quiet time around the house. I still remember reading classics like Jack London's *Call of the Wild*, Edwin O'Connor's *The Last Hurrah*, J.D. Salinger's *Catcher in the Rye* and Harper Lee's *To Kill a Mockingbird* during summers as a St. Ignatius student in the 1960s.

Swimming: Sadly, the seven-pool swimming facilities at Sutro's closed in early 1954 (more than a decade prior to the closure of the museum and its subsequent fire) due to maintenance issues. By the 1960s, San Francisco neighborhoods were dotted with public swimming pools, and the venerable (but ice-cold) Fleishhacker Pool was still in operation adjacent to the San Francisco Zoo. Summertime swim lessons were offered at the Jewish Community Center, several YMCA locations and private swim clubs.

The End: Summer would inevitably wind down, often with a family Labor Day outing—one last sweet taste of freedom. That night, just as the temperatures were beginning to warm up in San Francisco, tens of thousands of youngsters carefully laid out clothes and school supplies and went to bed early, trying to prepare for the new school year that was set to begin.

Those really were the "good old days" that so many people miss today.

The Jewish Community Center at California Street and Presidio Avenue, 1948. This corner was the western terminus of the California Street Cable Railroad until the line was cut back to Van Ness Avenue in 1956. The JCC opened a new building here in 1994. *OpenSFHistory.*

A vintage license plate frame recalls the grand era of swimming at Sutro's from 1896 to 1954. The museum and skating rink remained open for a dozen more years and closed just prior to the June 1966 fire that destroyed the empty structure. *Glenn D. Koch collection.*

16

The New City Emerges

I n just the first twenty years of the current century/millennium, a new city has begun to emerge, with developments sometimes taking longtime residents by surprise as some old venues drastically change; several entire neighborhoods are in the midst of complete makeovers. Here are just a few examples of the new San Francisco that is emerging.

Bayview–Hunters Point: The original commercial shipyard with dry dock facilities opened in 1870 and long defined the industrial character of the adjacent area. After the facility was taken over by the federal government prior to World War II, the navy operated the facility until 1974, when it was closed as part of a base reduction plan. A massive cleanup program took place before the first new private housing units opened in 2010, although since then, concerns have surfaced regarding the need for additional abatement work. Throughout the neighborhood, there are increasing examples of government/corporate investment, including the new T–Third Street streetcar line (with revenue service that began in 2007), a new Lowe's that opened on Bayshore Boulevard in 2010, the expansion and refurbishment of the historic 1888 Opera House and the arrival of other businesses, including national retail chains. The area surrounding the former Candlestick Park (a.k.a. 3Com Park and Monster Park, for two of its short-lived corporate sponsors) has been slated for housing and neighborhood commercial development.

de Young Museum: The original de Young Museum opened in Golden Gate Park in 1895 as an offshoot of the Midwinter Fair of 1894 and was

The new de Young Museum's observation tower provides spectacular views of the entire city and may be accessed for free by the public during the building's regular hours of operation. *WolfmanSF photo/Wikimedia Commons.*

housed in a building on the grounds of that exposition. Badly damaged in 1906, it was closed for repairs but eventually reopened. Through Michael de Young's efforts, a new building was constructed in 1919 and expanded in 1921 and 1925, and the original structure was declared unsafe and demolished in 1929. In the years following World War II, the ornate ornamentation of the original de Young was removed after it was found that the salt air was corroding the supporting steel rods. The 1989 Loma Prieta earthquake caused severe damage to the building, and plans were developed for a new museum. Voters twice defeated bond measures to fund a new museum, though supporters led fundraising efforts that were successful, and the new de Young Museum opened in October 2005. There was initially some public resistance to the new design, although as the copper exterior is softened by the elements, the design has achieved a growing acceptance.

Mission Bay: Today's Mission Bay neighborhood was once home to a sprawling combination of industrial buildings, warehouses, railroad tracks and switching yards. In 1998, the Board of Supervisors declared the neighborhood a redevelopment area, and Southern Pacific railroad sold most of its extensive holdings to developers. Once Caltrain Peninsula commute service became the primary user of the tracks, surplus land was sold for development. In this millennium, the neighborhood has rapidly become an employment center for hospital and health care services, as well as biotechnology research and development. New housing, both rental and owned, and for individuals at all income levels, has been and is continuing to be built. New public facilities, including police and fire stations and the newest branch of San Francisco Public Library, are already in service.

A 2015 aerial view of San Francisco from an unusual angle looking from east to west. Golden Gate Park is visible at upper right in the distance, and the Bay Bridge is at lower right. Mission Bay is in the center foreground, and the Golden Gate Bridge is out of camera range at far right. *Alfred Twu photo.*

Neighborhood retail is continuing to expand to serve the shopping and dining needs of tens of thousands of new residents.

POPOS: Privately-owned public open spaces (POPOS) are publicly accessible spaces such as plazas, terraces, atriums, small parks and snippets that are provided and maintained by private developers. Most POPOS locations are in the downtown office district area and have been created as part of new requirements introduced in the 1985 Downtown Plan. Street-level signage—used to identify amenities such as accessibility, seating capacity, food service and restrooms—is continuing to become more universal.

Salesforce Terminal: The five-level structure opened to the public in August 2018 as a replacement for the old Transbay Terminal, which was built in 1939 and damaged by the 1989 Loma Prieta earthquake. The top level features an open public park, and the next level down offers bus service by several MUNI and AC Transit lines, plus a bus link to Amtrak's Emeryville station in the East Bay. The main level includes retail space and public art, plus street access for pedestrians and access for cabs and ride-sharing services. The first subterranean level is a public concourse with additional retail outlets. The lowest level has been planned to include a new station for Caltrain service to the peninsula. A station for California's planned high-speed rail service was also part of the original site plan, though that project has recently come under increased financial scrutiny by Governor Gavin Newsom. The new $2.2 billion structure was closed to the public six weeks

Official signage for privately owned public open spaces (POPOS) in San Francisco. *Author's collection.*

after opening to allow for an investigation of cracks in certain steel beams, with a quiet reopening taking place on July 1, 2019.

San Francisco State University: The school moved to its Lake Merced campus just in time for the start of the 1953–54 school year, when the new site was home to 5,000 students. Since then, the campus has significantly expanded, and by 1965, facilities had more than doubled from a decade earlier through additions to the original buildings and construction of the Psychology building. Enrollment soon reached 10,000 students. In 1972, the school was upgraded to university status, with many additional programs. Six more buildings were added in the early 1970s, and the number of enrolled students surpassed 20,000 for the first time. The 1980s and '90s saw major new Humanities and Associated Students Children's Center buildings, an addition to the Arts and Industry building and renovation of the Cesar Chavez Student Center. Student housing and parking remained serious issues for the campus as the new millennium approached. As the school continued growing (with 27,000 students and 3,000-plus faculty/staff by the year 2000), additional parking and residential facilities were added on the west side of campus. A major library expansion in 2008 and a massive new

186

Picture taken from Salesforce Terminal, looking west. The four-story (plus two underground levels) structure runs for nearly three full city blocks between Minna and Natoma Streets (just south of Mission Street) and west from Beale Street nearly to 2nd Street. *Fullmetal2887 photo/Wikimedia Commons.*

Mashouf Wellness Center, opened in 2017, are serving a growing student population of well over 30,000, and the school is now awarding more than 7,000 degrees each year.

South-of-Market Housing: In the 1930s and '40s, much of the housing in the area consisted of single-occupancy rooms rented to laborers and seagoing workers. The City had a redevelopment plan for the neighborhood by 1953, and by the 1970s, major corporations such as Bank of America, General Electric and Pacific Telephone were expanding their operations into new buildings. The opening of the Moscone Convention Center in 1981 was a huge change for the area, and many building sites that had been vacant since the 1970s began to sprout new upscale residential towers and developments. Today, open space is at a premium as multiple high-rise condos began to appear, including Millennium Tower, which is currently being worked on to correct structural issues related to settling. Numerous new large-scale projects are currently planned.

Valencia Street at 18th Street, looking north to Cathedral Hill in 2012 during the "Sunday Streets" program intended to limit vehicles and provide greater public access for one day per week. *Max Kirkeberg collection.*

Sunday Streets: In the late 1960s, the city began closing the entire eastern portion of Main Drive (now John F. Kennedy Drive) in Golden Gate Park to vehicular traffic on Sundays. The program was an instant success and continues today, more than fifty years later. Sunday Streets was developed beginning in 2008 as a joint venture of the nonprofit Livable City in partnership with various city agencies. Ten events are held each year, with routes ranging from one to four miles in length and traffic-free walkable spaces that include fun, free activities provided by local nonprofits, community groups and small businesses. Routes are planned in advance in diverse neighborhood locations throughout San Francisco.

Treasure Island: Constructed and originally occupied by the 1939–40 Golden Gate International Exposition, this site became the longtime home to a large U.S. Naval Station. Following the closure of the base in 1997, the federal government ceded the property to the City and County of San Francisco. As cleanup and refurbishment progresses, more than 1,800 San Franciscans are already living in existing rental townhomes and apartments on the island. Future plans include new housing (both rental and owned) on Treasure Island and also on parts of adjacent Yerba Buena Island. It is estimated that by the year 2030, there will be 8,000-plus new units—both affordable and market-rate—with a population of 20,000 to 25,000 residents.

ᴀ Glimpse into the Future

I n addition to several major projects already completed by 2018–19, many more that will change the face of San Francisco remain on the drawing board. Nearly two dozen new high-rise structures have received Planning Department approval and are already in some phase of construction in several neighborhoods, including Civic Center, the Financial District, South-of-Market and Mission Bay.

The Salesforce Terminal, opened in 2018, is now often regarded as the focal point of its own new neighborhood—known as the Transit District—with at least five new high-rise buildings already planned for the 500 block of Howard Street. Many of these include housing units (for persons of various income levels), some offices and ground-floor commercial spaces.

Among the other major projects being developed across the city are the following:

BART: The governing board of directors, as well as daily riders, have long been aware that the system's capacity has been stretched thin since the turn of the millennium. Now, twenty years later, plans are slowly being formulated to address the matter.

The original system was extended to Pittsburg/Antioch and Dublin/ Pleasanton in the East Bay in the late 1990s and to Oakland Airport in 2014. Service was extended directly into San Francisco International Airport in 2003.

Today, BART faces new challenges—earthquake retrofits, new rolling stock, and further line expansions to accommodate shifting population centers.

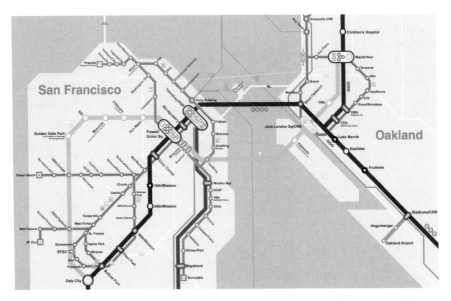

A vision of existing (and some potential new) transit alignments, including a second BART tube beneath San Francisco Bay, with a new line running west beneath Geary to Golden Gate Park before turning south through the Sunset District and beneath 19th Avenue on the western side of San Francisco. Also shown are existing (and some potential new) MUNI streetcar lines. *Adam Susaneck image.*

Among service enhancements within San Francisco are several projects included in a plan known as BART 2050. One is a second Transbay Tube that would allow for more frequent train service to/from the East Bay. As this new route enters the city from Alameda, its first stop might be at 3rd and King Streets, where it would offer a connection to the Central Subway (set to open in 2019), then another stop at Powell Street/Union Square before extending west beneath Geary, with potential stations at Van Ness Avenue, Fillmore Street/ Japantown Center, Masonic Avenue/USF and 6th Avenue, and veering south to stations at Golden Gate Park–Museums, 19th and Judah, 19th and Taraval and a major hub at Stonestown/Parkmerced/SFSU before rejoining the main Peninsula line at Daly City station. Other projects involve improved pedestrian connectivity between the existing Embarcadero Station and the new Transbay Transit Center and an infill station at 30th and Mission Streets.

While these BART expansions in San Francisco are slated for well into the future, it is clear that the time for discussions and planning has already arrived.

Central Subway: As an expansion of the T–Third Street MUNI streetcar line, which opened in 2007, construction of the Central Subway began in 2010, with completion now anticipated to occur by early 2020. With a new alignment, T-line MUNI trains will stop at the Caltrain station at 4th and King Streets, then proceed north on 4th Street, with a surface station at 4th and Brannan. Proceeding north on 4th Street, streetcars will then enter a subway, with underground stations at Yerba Buena/Moscone Center, Union Square and Chinatown. Tunneling has been completed as far as North Beach for future expansion, including possible extensions to the Northern Waterfront, the Marina and the Presidio. Although some residents questioned the route when it was approved in 2008, recent construction in Mission Bay—both residential and that of large employers such as UCSF and affiliated health care providers and research centers—has confirmed the wisdom of the route and its possibilities for the future.

Chase Center: The NBA's Golden State Warriors team arrived in San Francisco in 1962 and played locally but made a move to the Oakland Coliseum in 1971. With expanded construction opportunities in the new Mission Bay neighborhood, an alliance with JPMorgan Chase was announced in 2016, and construction on the new Chase Center began in January 2017. The Warriors' new home will have 18,000 seats, a theatre, over half a million square feet of office and lab space and 100,000 square feet of retail space. The privately financed project is set for completion in the 2019–20 basketball season.

Fort Scott: The largest remaining parcel open for development within the Presidio grounds covers thirty acres and contains twenty-two buildings. The site was originally developed in 1912 and remained in military use until the decommissioning of the Presidio in 1994. Managed by the Presidio Trust, a federal agency charged with operating the 1,191-acre site without taxpayer support, Fort Scott relies upon funds earned through leasing homes, workspaces, hotels, a golf course and event venues. In 2019, directors of the group will be selecting tenants and philanthropic groups to plan the redevelopment of this final space within the Presidio grounds.

India Basin: Nearly 1,600 new homes, 200,000 square feet of commercial space, and fifteen acres of parklands are planned for the shoreline area just north of Hunters Point.

Mission Rock: Nearly thirty acres of parking and storage facilities near the Giants South-of-Market ballpark are planned for conversion into more than 1,500 rental apartments and well over one million square feet of commercial space, plus open parkland in the area of 3rd Street, Terry Francois Boulevard, Mission Rock Street and Pier 48.

Moscone Center: Opened in 1981, the convention center has been expanded multiple times. The most recent renovation—a $551 million, four-year project—was completed in early 2019. The facility now has nearly 1.4 million square feet of rentable space in its three buildings, which are connected by a glass skybridge over Howard Street.

Parkmerced: Developed and built as low-rise garden apartments by the Metropolitan Life Insurance Company in the years before World War II and expanded with eleven new apartment towers in 1950, the community has passed through the hands of many corporate owners since the 1970s. It was determined by the current owner that the older garden units were suffering from decades of deferred maintenance and that demolition of the old units and replacement with larger units was the preferred option. A long-range plan presented to the Board of Supervisors was approved in 2011 and sustained after numerous court challenges. Work is set to begin in 2019 and will continue until 2040, with current tenants being accommodated (and current rent controls remaining in place for them) in existing tower

Architectural plans show a new Parkmerced after all 1,538 low-rise garden apartments are replaced with 5,679 new units in mid-rise tower buildings. The eleven existing high-rise towers dating from 1950 will remain, resulting in 8,900 homes by the year 2040—triple the size of the community in 2019. *Rogelio Foronda/Parkmerced Vision.*

apartments and/or new mid-rise units to be built on open space in the development prior to any demolitions.

Potrero Power Plant: The old natural gas and diesel electric power plant, which began operations in the 1890s and was decommissioned in 2010, once had the capacity to produce a full one-third of San Francisco's peak-time electrical needs, but San Francisco now receives power from a variety of sources throughout the State of California, including Hetch Hetchy. The twenty-one-acre shoreline site on Illinois Street has now been opened for development of five million square feet of mixed-use space, including owned and rental housing (both market-rate and affordable), restaurants, retail shops and a hotel, with the old three-hundred-foot stack preserved as an architectural centerpiece.

San Francisco State University Future Growth: Construction is already underway on a massive new Liberal and Creative Arts Building just west of the 1950s Broadcast and Electronic Communication Arts (BECA) Building on Holloway Drive, with completion set for late 2020. At the same time, construction has also begun at the corner of Varela Avenue and Holloway Drive (just off 19th Avenue and opposite the SFSU Library), where several blocks of former Parkmerced garden apartments sold to SFSU in 2005 for student housing have now been demolished and are being replaced with a compound of six-story student residential structures with ground-floor retail tenants.

Schlage Lock: For nearly seventy-five years (from 1926 to 1999), Schlage Lock operated a large industrial facility on Bayshore Boulevard in Visitacion Valley. As of the mid-1970s, the firm had a workforce of 1,600 and was the largest manufacturing company operating in San Francisco at the time. Just prior to the turn of the millennium, the facility was sold, with headquarters and operations moving to Colorado. Most of the site was cleared beginning in 2009, with the exception of the classic red-Mission-tiled office building, which has been preserved for new uses. Once the environmental cleanup of the land is completed, plans call for a new mixed-use, transit-oriented neighborhood with nearly 1,700 new homes.

San Francisco churches, notably Glide Memorial Methodist and St. Boniface, both in the Tenderloin neighborhood, have long offered support services to local residents in need. Father Alfred Boeddeker (*far left*), founder of St. Anthony's Dining Room, is shown with two volunteers and the chef serving food at the then-new facility in 1950. The dining room recently expanded to a new building just across the street and serves nearly 1 million meals annually, 365 days per year, to needy San Franciscans of all ages—men, women and children. *San Francisco History Center/San Francisco Public Library.*

18

Giving Thanks through the Years

N ow that I have threescore-and-a-bunch of Thanksgiving holidays under my belt (both figuratively and literally), it's time to take a look back at the subtle changes that have taken place in celebration rituals over the years.

Before my parents were married, Dad's family enjoyed Thanksgiving dinners at Grison's on Van Ness Avenue—a popular restaurant from the 1930s through the 1970s where management even provided guests with a box for taking home all the leftovers from each table's turkey and side dishes. By the 1950s, though, they were celebrating at his family's home on 21ˢᵗ Avenue in the Parkside. Mom's relatives, on the other hand, had been gathering around her parents' dining room table in the Mission District for every Thanksgiving dinner since her childhood.

In the early years of their marriage, my parents alternated between the two groups—a pattern that continued for some time. Once I arrived on the scene, my parents established a firm rule—we continued to spend Thanksgiving with relatives but always stayed at home for Christmas and Easter, since it was too difficult to separate a young child from his just-opened gifts and chocolate eggs.

One of my grandmothers was a better cook than the other—something that became clearer to me over time. And while one of them permitted guests a beverage before dinner, along with a small dish of nuts, olives and cheese-stuffed celery on the coffee table, the other imposed a fasting ritual that would have strained the most fervent religious zealots. In her opinion, even a single cup of morning coffee was sure to "ruin your appetite for dinner."

Each grandmother emptied her linen closet and china cabinet to set an amazing table. Freshly ironed tablecloths and napkins were standard, along with large china dinner plates and an array of sparkling glassware surrounded by more candles than at the Vatican. There were enough utensils laid out to dig another Panama Canal, and while one of my grandmothers put out multiple sets of salt and pepper shakers, the other made all seasoning decisions in the privacy of her kitchen.

Both grandmothers grew up in the era of coal and wood stoves, so it was no surprise that the time required to roast a turkey was highly subjective, even though both of them had been using modern-era gas ranges since well before I was born. (My personal preference today is simple—about fifteen minutes per pound at 325 degrees and covered with foil until the final hour.) There was the perennial debate over mashed potatoes (one favored smooth and the other preferred tiny bits of lump) as the cook and her helpers huddled over the oven, poking and probing the bird, while Dad stood by, patiently holding his trusty carving knife—which was updated to an electric version after 1965.

At one house, it was just a small group of immediate family at the table, while the other grandmother included her four children and their three spouses, plus seven grandchildren, a few of her own siblings and their spouses and a variety of cousins—many of us overflowing to the "children's table." Much of my interest in genealogy began once I was seated with the grown-ups, where I learned firsthand the difference between a second cousin once removed and a third cousin, recognizing that I had some very nice ones in both categories. Place cards, if not actual name badges, were essential, and conversations ran the gamut of Chevy vs. Ford, employee benefits in civil service vs. private industry and which cousin once came home from the office Christmas party and then fell headlong into the tree while adjusting the star.

Until the late 1960s, dress codes of the era dictated neckties for men and dresses for ladies, but that's where the resemblance to the Norman Rockwell Thanksgiving dinner table scene ended. Each grandmother "dished up" in the kitchen, making her own decisions about various portion sizes for each guest, which ones preferred light vs. dark meat and precise quantities of mashed potatoes, dressing and vegetables (always frozen peas and carrots boiled to death) for each of us. The only choices to be made by guests at the table were in regard to gravy, rolls

Norma Braiverman selling turkey to customers at Crystal Palace Market at 8th and Market Streets, 1953. The Crystal Palace contained dozens of individual merchants selling fresh and packaged groceries, household products, home decor items and more—all under one roof. *San Francisco History Center/San Francisco Public Library.*

and cranberry sauce—Ocean Spray jellied, served on a small crystal dish, which never held any other food. That dish, which is now over one hundred years old, is still in use on my own table.

One grandmother was a teetotaler, with the strongest liquid in her kitchen being a bottle of vanilla extract. The other grandmother, who had an ongoing friendship with some retired Christian Brothers, was always in possession of a few bottles of wine—gifted to her in exchange for regular packages of chocolate chip cookies and banana bread that she would ship to them in Napa County.

Both grandmothers served apple pie and pumpkin pie for dessert—made from scratch by one and purchased from the Different Bakery on Taraval by the other. Whipped cream and service à la mode were essentials at one house, and at the other, these were considered to be excesses that no one should expect after such a filling meal.

Sadly, by 1970, both of my grandmothers were gone. Mom's sister began hosting Thanksgiving at her sixth-floor apartment in Stonestown and immediately relaxed the dress code—no more neckties required for men, and women could wear slacks. She also ditched the boiled peas and carrots in favor of Stouffer's spinach soufflé and a corn casserole. Gewürztraminer and Riesling wines were substituted for Grandma's favorite Chateau La Salle (which always resembled a slightly alcoholic version of Welch's white grape juice with a generous dollop of sugar added). Mandarin orange Jell-O salad replaced the tossed green salad favored by one grandmother and the vegetable soup served by the other in earlier days, while *Sunset* magazine's "Artichoke Nibbles" were added to the selection of hors d'oeuvres. Those Thanksgiving meals throughout the 1970s and '80s still evoke memories of spectacular sunsets over Lake Merced before, during and after the meal, plus an ever-changing rotation of nonrelatives, many of whom became close family friends.

After my aunt's passing, Mom took over Thanksgiving when she was well past seventy. Even though she had never before hosted this holiday on her own, she was the hardworking assistant to others for years. I remember taking her to Petrini's at Stonestown to pick out a turkey, and she definitely put the staff through a rigorous workout—"too small/bad shape/too heavy to lift" were just a few of her criticisms. One butcher finally solved the problem by gently suggesting that she buy two medium-sized, perfectly shaped birds, then roast them side by side—problem solved!

Guests now included a few of Mom's cousins and some of Dad's cousins, too. One year, out of deference to picky eaters, Mom declared Thanksgiving to be a buffet and laid out all the traditional dishes in the kitchen so that everyone could help themselves to desired portions of what they liked best before sitting down in the dining room. This method also accommodated second helpings, plus the erratic schedules of some guests who might be delayed because of volunteering to serve food at a shelter or by late-running high school football action at Kezar Stadium. At the end of that first year's experiment, everyone agreed that serving dinner buffet-style was great.

Just before the turn of the millennium, we began accepting invitations from cousins and some longtime family friends who lived in the Wine Country. This turned the holiday into a long-weekend excursion, and that considerably pleased Mom—plus, she did not have to worry about cleaning up afterward. She even came home with some new recipes, including one for lemon meringue pie from our late cousin Kathy. The palate-cleansing properties of lemon are so good after a heavy meal that I still give a silent nod to my cousin by always having one of her pies among the desserts. Once she got home, Mom's first task was always roasting a stuffed turkey so that there would be enough "leftovers" for sandwiches over the weekend and then a big pot of soup.

In this millennium, I rotate between accepting invitations from family and friends and playing host at my home for Thanksgiving. Many years of being "assistant helper" has given me a fairly good repertoire of recipes, although just for the record, I will admit to a culinary mishap or two—like the year that I served a colorful but too spicy carrot soup from a recipe that I found on a can of ground black pepper (that should have been a tip-off!) or the time that one guest brought a pumpkin pie made with honey instead of sugar, which resulted in a thick, syrupy filling inside a very soggy crust. The moral of the story is: Always have a backup plan for an essential dish that does not turn out correctly *and* know the location and holiday hours of the nearest neighborhood grocery store for last-minute emergencies.

Thanksgivings spent as a guest at someone else's table remind me of side dishes that I have never been able to successfully prepare at home—the perfect cornbread muffins, a spectacular casserole of Brussels sprouts with bacon, hollowed-out orange shells filled with a creamy sweet potato mixture. Each year, I continue to experiment, hoping to re-create some of these memorable recipes.

As for serving, I began to notice a long time ago that Thanksgiving foods taste better when reheated, so I now roast the turkey and prepare the side dishes one day before the holiday, then let everything cool. Once the turkey is sliced and arranged on platters, I cover and refrigerate everything, then clean up the enormous mess and relax, knowing that the entire meal is ready to go and just needs to be warmed up. So far, after more than a decade following this routine, there have been no complaints from guests, and I get to spend more time with them in the living room instead of working in the kitchen. In the years that I'm at someone else's table for the holiday, I still roast a small turkey at home so that there will be a generous supply of leftovers for sandwiches.

Today, the linen napkins and lace tablecloths of the past have faded into history, and I use a washable, nonwrinkle tablecloth/napkin set with an autumn leaf pattern that hides red wine stains. There is just a single orange candle as the centerpiece, and wine glasses are the sturdy survivors from a set of stemware given to my parents at the time of their 1947 wedding. One unmolded can of Ocean Spray is displayed on that small crystal dish, although nowadays there is also a more adventuresome homemade version of cranberry sauce alongside it.

Over the last few years, I've begun noticing a tendency by some people to include holiday décor—complete with holly, twinkling lights and decorated trees—in mid-November. This is "holiday creep"—and creepy it is. But for some families, with multiple relatives clamoring for their presence at various year-end celebrations, this has become a workable solution for many to resolve holiday conflicts by celebrating multiple events—Thanksgiving, Hanukkah, Christmas, New Year's Eve—all together.

The most memorable celebrations seem to come soon after the loss of a loved one. In those years, there is often some reshuffling of the guest list—the dearly departed, perhaps someone else unable to travel and, occasionally, some missing younger folks away at college or off on their own. At the same time, new guests appear—those whose plans shifted at the last minute, along with new friends and perhaps some recently acquired fiancés, spouses, babies and significant others joining us for the first time and often setting a new tradition for years to come.

Each time the group changes, we shift gears and welcome newcomers, sharing our traditions with them and listening attentively to their cherished holiday remembrances as we all give thanks—because that's what this holiday is all about.

19

Just Like the Ones I Used to Know

In earlier times, holidays were celebrated one by one, with little or no overlap. Halloween items might go on sale in early October at local retailers such as Vicente Variety at 23rd and Vicente, King Norman's on Clement Street, many local Woolworth stores and dozens of other places. When that holiday was over, Thanksgiving goods appeared, and Christmas merchandise would follow a month later. It was a pleasant, orderly way to do business—unlike in many stores today, where back-to-school and Halloween items are often displayed side-by-side in mid-July, with Christmas-themed goods sometimes sliding into the mix before Labor Day.

It used to be not until just after Thanksgiving that TV commercials began advertising Schwinn bicycles, Easy-Bake ovens, boxed games, dolls and Lionel trains as Christmas/Hanukkah gifts "for good girls and boys"—a qualifier seldom seen today. Moms and dads were expected to overhear such suggestions, and most kids helped in the process with some not-too-subtle reminders and lengthy letters to Santa. My mother (along with many others who had secretarial training) kept her holiday shopping list in shorthand—a secret code that was indecipherable to dads and kids.

On December 1, local newspapers began placing a prominent box on their front pages to announce "Only 23 more shopping days before Christmas," while big stores politely refrained from placing a Santa Claus face in a corner of their daily ads until Thanksgiving was over. The jolly man's arrival downtown via cable car was a cause for celebration—unlike today's public stampede and trampling of other greedy shoppers in big-

Emporium department store on Market Street decorated for Christmas in 1974. *Frank Florianz photo.*

box stores just hours after Thanksgiving dinner as weary rent-a-cops look on helplessly.

Holiday shopping trips followed a pattern for many families. The Emporium on Market Street was often the first place visited. Five streetcar lines and numerous MUNI buses stopped right in front of the store, and often, more than half the passengers simultaneously disembarked. The store was decorated to look like a winter wonderland, including its massive toy department at the back of the fourth floor, with children's clothing nearby. Families would often split up, with Grandma or another relative taking the kids to visit Santa and the carnival-like roof rides so moms could shop on their own.

Lunch at Woolworth across the street was a regular stop for many families, and that store offered numerous gift items priced under one dollar (records, books, picture frames, desk accessories) for bargain-conscious shoppers—especially school-age children. Others favored a sit-down lunch at Bernstein's on Powell Street, John's Grill on Ellis or Townsend's on Geary—particularly if grandparents happened to be present.

A visit to the City of Paris tree beneath the rotunda was a big part of the day, and most kids insisted on viewing the spectacular ornaments from each floor in order to see the details. Depending on how well everyone's feet were feeling, there might be a walk through the Podesta-Baldocchi flower shop on Grant Avenue, with thousands of tiny twinkling lights, poinsettias and the scent of evergreen boughs. Ladies might make a stop at the beautifully appointed restrooms of I. Magnin, and if youngsters were especially well-behaved, there might even be a sweet treat at Blum's before the streetcar ride home, with everyone feeling exhausted but happy.

Many people also made excursions to Stonestown (more roof rides at the Emporium store there), plus shopping at B. Dalton Books, Gallenkamp Shoes or Toy World. At the far end of the mall was the Butler Brothers store—which became City of Paris in 1960, then Bullock's in 1977 and Nordstrom in 1988 (Nordstrom is now under internal scrutiny by its corporate owners for a possible closure). Other visits might include GETs on Sloat Boulevard (kids' clothing, Kodak camera equipment, and discounted toys), Sears at Geary and Masonic (tools for Dad/a major appliance for Mom) or one of the numerous shops along neighborhood shopping corridors. Although we generally carried our purchases home, today, many customers rely upon a friendly UPS or FedEx driver to deliver items from online merchants.

In terms of childhood traditions, many of us continued to express belief in Santa out of fear that our gifts might become underwear, bathrobes or slippers if our parents suspected that we knew the truth. As we grew older, wish-list items shifted from toys and games to very specific clothing and accessories. Parents often found it difficult to judge fashion trends, and many of them relied upon anything from Joseph Magnin to please teenage girls and items from Bruce Bary in Stonestown to please boys (I still wear the red-and-blue scarf—in S.I. colors—that came from that store on Christmas in 1966). Eventually, money became a popular gift that accommodated changing teenage tastes.

Major stores offered gift certificates, but there was nowhere near today's proliferation of gift cards. In the old days, my parents might stock up with a couple of one-pound boxes of See's Candy or gift-wrapped quarts of bourbon as last-minute gifts—today, a quick visit to any supermarket provides easy access to gift cards from hundreds of different stores and restaurants.

Mom always picked our family's Christmas card in November—invariably, it was one with a decorated tree in shades of green and gold. (Since college, I've favored images of the three kings for my own cards.) On a Sunday afternoon in December, there would be an assembly line at the kitchen table—Mom addressing envelopes (using Palmer Method penmanship from her Catholic school days), while Dad would write messages to a dozen or so of his World War II Navy buddies scattered across the country, and I would apply stamps, return address labels and Christmas seals. December mail was delivered twice a day until the mid-1960s, and all the cards we received were displayed throughout the living room and dining room.

Among Jewish families, Hanukkah shares the seasonal calendar with Christmas. The eight-day holiday commemorates the rededication of the Second Temple in Jerusalem. At that time, there was only enough oil to keep the lights on the menorah (a Hebrew word meaning "candelabrum") burning for a single day, yet the flames continued flickering for eight nights, leaving time to secure a fresh oil supply. This miracle inspired Jewish leaders to proclaim a yearly eight-day "Festival of Lights," and the lighting of candles on the menorah remains an essential part of the tradition.

In families with young children, Hanukkah celebrations might be spread across the full eight nights. Since the candles represent ancient lamp oil,

Shepherds, "The Three Wise Men" Golden Gate Park ©1955 - N. Blair

The San Francisco Council of Churches sponsored a "Living Nativity Scene" at Lindley Meadow in Golden Gate Park in the 1950s and 1960s. Rehearsal took place during daylight hours in advance of scheduled nightly performances held under floodlights. *San Francisco History Center/San Francisco Public Library.*

foods prepared in oil, such as potato pancakes (latkes) and doughnuts, are traditional celebratory Hanukkah foods. Families with older children sometimes opted for an abbreviated version of events, with songs, holiday foods and gifting only on the first night, then simply lighting one additional candle each night for the rest of the week.

On the 2600 block of 18th Avenue, adults and kids alike were eagerly awaiting the second Saturday of December—the kickoff of an annual outdoor holiday lighting tradition that started in the 1930s, when the homes were new, and continued until 1969–70. This was the night that my grandmother always took us out for an early dinner at the Hot House so that party preparations in Mom's kitchen were not disturbed. Mexican food, salt spray on a cold night, twinkling lights and the joyful sounds of Playland remain an indelible Christmastime memory for me.

Once we were home after dinner, Santa would arrive at 6:00 p.m., courtesy of the San Francisco Fire Department, via an engine from the station on 18th Avenue near Rivera. As sirens blared, all the Christmas trees and outdoor lights on the block were illuminated at the same time. Even those who did not celebrate the religious aspects of Christmas joined in with lighted outdoor Stars of David plus festive pinecone wreaths and jolly snow figures in their windows.

As loudspeakers played carols, Santa sat on a gold-painted "throne" at someone's garage entrance, listening to wish lists and distributing peppermint candy canes. The festivities continued with open house parties up and down both sides of the street—parents, kids, classmates, relatives and friends all joining together in a wonderful celebration that spilled in and out of every home until nearly midnight. We truly knew our neighbors then, and many of those friendships continue to this day.

As the holidays grew closer, baking was a popular activity, and neighborhood grocery stores sometimes experienced shortages of essential items. Many moms, including mine, would begin accumulating cereals and seasonings for her Chex mix as others stocked up on red and green sprinkles, chocolate chips, walnuts or the makings for Rice Krispies treats. Many households saved empty jars and boxes all year long for holiday packaging, eventually filling them with food treats wrapped in shiny foil and topped with a red or green bow as presents for neighbors.

Last-minute gifts (Dad's traditional bottle of Aqua Velva aftershave and a carton of Kool menthol cigarettes—what *were* we thinking?) could be picked up at Reis' Pharmacy on Taraval Street. This was also the place to replenish those red/green/silver foil-wrapped Hershey's Kisses that were being quietly devoured daily.

For more than fifty years, my father's aunt hosted a Christmas Eve gathering in her big flat on Duboce Avenue, where her youngest child/grandchild/great-grandchild recited "The Night Before Christmas"—an event that I still remember from its final days in the mid-1950s.

Most families with children opened gifts on Christmas morning, giving parents extra time to agonize over the horrors of "easy-to-assemble" bicycles with strangely worded instructions: "attach rail YX to crossbar L-113, tightening with prudent care to avoid any accidentals which may lead to injurious catastrophes."

As kids grew older, many families shifted gift exchanges to Christmas Eve. By the 1970s, many people had shifted to a tradition of appetizers/drinks, then opening presents, followed by dessert and coffee. Among my high school and college friends, this celebration was often extended by attending Midnight Mass at St. Ignatius Church—a popular site for this traditional service since the 1880s, when it was located on Hayes near Van Ness. Revelers might then return home around 1:30 a.m. to continue the festivities, often in one of those knotty pine downstairs rooms.

Christmas morning breakfast was another popular tradition. Although the Cliff House and its gin fizzes attracted crowds, many people preferred home-based celebrations with made-from-scratch baked goods, sparkling cider, a variety of sausages and hot chocolate on the table. Everyone was then free to sleep in and to relax over breakfast/brunch while still clad in nightclothes—a wardrobe statement still favored by all of my cousins when we gather together.

In many families, Christmas dinner resembled a replay of Thanksgiving, though with many more red/green foods (Jell-O salads, veggies, desserts). Often centered on a turkey, rib roast or ham (plus fresh seafood among Italian families), this meal was another traditional event. Among those families who opened their gifts on Christmas Eve, some opted for a more casual dinner with a smaller number of guests on Christmas Day—giving college-age kids who happened to be home on school break a chance to socialize with their contemporaries.

Today, many family members live far beyond San Francisco, so the holidays have evolved into a two-week-long calendar of events, with visiting, gift exchanges and celebratory meals among parents, stepparents, siblings, stepsiblings, in-laws, ex-in-laws, cousins and multiple sets of grandparents/step-grandparents. Instead of a few days of festivities, gatherings are now

As on many neighborhood shopping streets throughout San Francisco, West Portal Avenue merchants decorated brightly for the season in 1947. *OpenSFHistory.*

spread out, with a significant increase in the amount of driving involved, thus introducing many holiday bottlenecks—at 19th Avenue, the Golden Gate and Bay Bridges, US 101, and Interstate 280, to name just a few.

Still, with a spirit of goodwill in the air, and regardless of one's religious convictions, most people would agree that the end of the calendar year and the start of winter is a fine time to extend good wishes to one and all, along with hopes for a very happy new year.

In the era after the 1906 fire, Mission Street became an important retail center while Market Street was undergoing reconstruction. Henry C. Hackett, a family-owned jewelry store, is shown here around 1912. Note the window sign that advertises "EYES EXAMINED"—a customary service offered by many jewelers during the era. *Christine Meagher Keller collection.*

20

A Case Study in Neighborhood Change

One of San Francisco's earliest neighborhoods, home to the Ohlone and Miwok tribes of Native Americans, the Mission District has almost certainly experienced more changes over a greater period of time than any other part of San Francisco.

1776–1810: For centuries, this area was a vast open space with marshlands—at least until the late 1700s. European settlers had begun developing the area by 1776, when Spanish Franciscan priests, acting on behalf of the government of Spain, established Mission Dolores. The present Mission building was constructed about a dozen years after the original site had been established. That move likely upset some people who might have complained about "changes in the neighborhood" that resulted in a slightly longer walk to church. Wetlands were routinely being filled and turned into "made ground"—a practice that would prove highly troublesome in the future. For many years, the Mission complex was part of a community of priests and Native Americans, engaged in farming and some light manufacturing, that continued to expand. Andrew Galvan, descended from an Ohlone Indian who was born in 1787 and baptized at Mission Dolores in 1801, has been curator at the Mission since January 2004. He makes note of two devastating changes in the early years of Mission life. The first was an epidemic, thought to be typhus, in 1795, and just eleven years later, in 1806, a widespread measles outbreak swept through the community. Galvan somberly notes: "Out of a population of 850 people, 343 died of measles in a period of thirty-six hours. Every child under the age of five died."

Mission Dolores was founded in 1776; a new adobe church was constructed at the current site in 1791, making it the oldest intact building in San Francisco. *Marco Zanoli photo.*

1810–1820: The Mexican War of Independence, an armed conflict between Mexico and Spain, began in 1810 at the height of the popularity of California's Mission system. During that time, more than one thousand people lived in or near Mission Dolores and were raising crops and livestock, with more than ten thousand cows and ten thousand sheep grazing in the area ranging from present-day 16th and Dolores Streets all the way to the current intersection of Mission and Cesar Chavez. Also during this time, some area residents were engaged in work such as wool processing and cloth manufacturing. Material shortages occurred during the war, as Spain was diverting provisions originally intended for the California Missions to other parts of its empire. As the war progressed, the Mission was once again on the cusp of drastic change.

1821–1847: The Mission way of life came to an end beginning in 1821, when Mexico became independent. The old Spanish missions began to fall into disrepair before being secularized (turned over to private owners) by the new Mexican government around 1834. That certainly represented a significant change in the lives of many people, and by the 1840s, the Native American population living at the Mission was nearly gone. Land grants placed most of Mission Dolores's holdings into private hands, and some new housing development occurred in the area.

1848–1874: The discovery of gold in Northern California in January 1848 brought tens of thousands of new residents into the area over the next few years, and many of them eventually came to San Francisco. Expanded roads and horse-car lines were built to link the downtown area of the city with the Mission, which had previously been connected only by dirt paths and a plank road. The area slowly evolved into a popular resort and entertainment district away from the congested downtown area, since it was located conveniently inland and distant from the fog and winds present near the Bay and ocean waters. Sporting events, gambling, saloons and various other forms of entertainment invaded the once-quiet landscape. One popular resort, The Willows, was situated just south of today's intersection of 18th and Mission Streets. A public entertainment grounds and zoo, Woodward's Gardens, which operated on a two-block parcel from 13th to 15th Streets between Mission and Valencia beginning in 1865, and an early sports complex, Recreation Grounds, opened in 1868 at the end of a streetcar line at 25th and Folsom at today's Garfield Square. The neighborhood was quite different from its rural incarnation from just twenty-five years earlier.

1875–1905: In the late nineteenth century, new waves of European immigrants began arriving and settling in the warm climate of the Mission District. The neighborhood, already almost exclusively Judeo-Christian, became home to primarily German and Irish immigrants (with younger generations often settling near their relatives), plus a large Scandinavian population located in the area north of Mission Dolores near the extended portion of Market Street between 15th and 16th Streets (where many of the older churches and buildings still have an affiliation and history that was originally Danish, Norwegian, Swedish or Finnish). The Mission was no longer rural, nor was it still agricultural or recreational in character. The addition of more and more paved roads and streetcar lines and the building of homes and businesses were factors that contributed to the transformation of the neighborhood. Even the once-popular resort, The Willows, had fallen from favor and was gone by the 1870s, with its site eventually buried beneath twenty feet of landfill as the ravines of the surrounding area were regraded to allow for additional housing and more transportation lines. Even the road passing by the front of Mission Dolores was altered around the time that a new redbrick parish church was added alongside the Mission to accommodate an increasing population. Instead of the Mission entrance being level with the roadway, as it had been for more than a century, later images confirm that the street, now named Dolores, was lowered considerably, and the front wall of the adjacent cemetery was moved back several feet as the old Mission itself acquired a set of several steps from the sidewalk to its front entrance. The excavated soil was then used to fill in parts of the nearby lake, Laguna de los Dolores, a few blocks away from 16th and Dolores Streets.

1906–1930: The events of 1906 ravaged much of San Francisco, leaving some 250,000 people homeless, though the Mission District, beyond 20th Street, was largely unscathed. Thanks to a continuous flow of water from a fire hydrant at 20th and Church Streets, the fire was stopped before it could move deep into the neighborhood. The South-of-Market neighborhood, once a bustling residential area, was completely obliterated on the first day of the fire, with thousands of residents walking into the nearby Mission District for safety and shelter; many of them eventually settled there permanently, including one set of this author's great-grandparents. Crowded as it already was with an immigrant population, the Mission also became a primary destination for those who had been displaced by the disaster. New homes and apartments were built, and the wood-framed Recreation Park, which seated 15,000 baseball fans, opened in 1907 bounded by 14th, Valencia, 15th and Guerrero Streets—a throwback to the neighborhood's earlier recreational character. For the next few decades, the term "bustling" was aptly applied to the once-tranquil Mission as thousands of new homes and businesses sprang up.

1931–1945: As time went on, these new Mission residents required more and more services. Mission Street itself became home to multiple streetcar lines, including some that headed south to San Mateo County. With Market Street still rebuilding as a result of the 1906 fire, Mission Street began a long period as a thriving retail corridor, even attracting shoppers from other neighborhoods. By the 1930s, the thoroughfare began to rival Market Street as home to a new phenomenon—the many large and glamorous movie palaces that were constructed during the heyday of Hollywood—and the shopping district itself became known throughout San Francisco as the "Mission Miracle Mile." In 1931, Seals Stadium,

The New Mission Theatre, circa 1968. Built in 1916 and renovated to its current style in 1932, the movie palace closed in 1993. For the next twenty years, the building operated as a discount furniture store, with the art deco sign remaining in place but in disrepair. The structure and its classic sign were revitalized as a movie house with food and beverage service and reopened in 2015. *Tom Gray photo/Jack Tillmany collection.*

located at 16th and Bryant Streets, replaced the old Recreation Park for minor-league baseball, initially with 16,000 seats and later expanded to nearly 23,000. Also in the early 1930s, parts of the old Mission cemetery, extending north to Church Street, were unceremoniously paved over for a schoolyard/parking lot. The Great Depression impacted the entire community as some older, large homes were subdivided into rooming houses at a time when many families had multiple generations, and sometimes boarders, living under the same roof. By the time of World War II, the Mission rivaled the core of Chinatown as the most densely packed neighborhood in San Francisco.

1946–1956: World War II and its aftermath brought about even more changes. With rentals at a premium during the war years, overcrowding in the postwar era caused many newlyweds to look for homes in locations that were less densely populated. Henry Doelger and other builders who had begun operations west of Twin Peaks in the 1930s were heavily advertising their new homes by 1946, luring tens of thousands of people from the overcrowded Mission District, including this author's mother, who was then a new bride. At the same time, various street widening projects in the Mission and adjacent areas (Clipper, Guerrero, South Van Ness, Army, Bayshore) offered easier routes to neighborhoods west of Twin Peaks, as well as to new suburban housing developments on the Peninsula.

1957–1967: By the late 1950s, the exodus of many younger people left a vacuum in San Francisco's housing supply that resulted in lower costs in the Mission (both rental and home ownership) as opposed to those in many other San Francisco neighborhoods. Seals Stadium was demolished after the opening of Candlestick Park in 1960, ending a long tradition of sporting venues in the neighborhood. Residential vacancies would soon be filled by a new wave of immigrants, initially from Mexico, then from Central and South America. Yet again, the Mission was changing. Average household incomes dipped, and many longtime Miracle Mile merchants closed or relocated and were replaced by businesses offering a different mix of goods and services to new residents.

1968–1998: BART construction in the late 1960s was viewed as a mixed blessing in the Mission. While it eventually improved transit time to and from downtown, the years of disruption caused by tunnel and station construction proved fatal to many of the remaining Mission Street merchants and the once-grand theatres (which were already endangered in most communities throughout the United States). By the 1970s, the Mission had begun to suffer from increases in crime and poverty. Fortunately, a group of neighborhood organizations banded together to fight the wholesale "urban renewal" that was then ravaging the Western Addition, so the Mission was able to escape the fate of wholesale demolition and rebuilding. Schools and houses of worship—along with health care providers, retailers and fraternal organizations—continued to evolve as the Mission stabilized once again and continued a long era as a thriving Hispanic neighborhood.

The fortieth annual Carnaval celebration in San Francisco took place in the Mission District in 2018. The annual two-day street parade and festival is a multicultural event held in May of each year as a fundraiser for community programs for children, youth, families and seniors. *Author's collection.*

1999–2009: The dawn of the new millennium began yet another period of tumultuous change. Many immigrant families from the 1960s had climbed the economic ladder and began settling in other communities beyond the Mission. The so-called "dot-com bubble" of 1997–2000 introduced a new element into the mix—the Internet employee. Mostly young and well educated people with a great familiarity with high-tech businesses, these newcomers began to settle into large Victorian and Edwardian homes and apartments throughout the Mission District, attracted by affordable rents and easy public transit into downtown San Francisco. One immediate change was the emergence of notably upscale bars and restaurants and the development of Valencia Street as a new "restaurant row" by the year 2000. While the original dot-com bubble later burst and was followed by the economic meltdown of 2007–2009, the Mission continued to be a peaceful enclave and home to a diverse population of both longtime residents and newcomers.

2010–present: The new rise of technology companies in the Bay Area began to put additional pressure on the Mission's economic stability after 2010. The well-educated, high-earning "techie" found the Mission to be a desirable location to settle, just as many other San Franciscans had in previous decades. This time, however, the newcomers were arriving with larger incomes and an ability to transform the neighborhood into something a bit more "bustling"—a word that has been used many times to describe the Mission. Today, open spaces such as Dolores Park are often jam-packed with humanity, sometimes leading to unpleasant exchanges. While some technology companies are headquartered in San Francisco, many others are located in San Mateo and Santa Clara counties, and several of the larger ones began running shuttle buses into the Mission and other San Francisco neighborhoods where large numbers of their employees were residing. These buses soon became the outward symbol of neighborhood antipathy toward newcomers. In addition, the rise in demolitions and new construction, owner move-ins and evictions of longtime tenants, fires of suspicious origin and overall gentrification of the area soon became problematic to many San Franciscans. The rising cost of housing in the Mission also extended into virtually every single neighborhood at the tip of the relatively tiny forty-nine-square-mile city where small homes (one thousand square feet) now routinely sell for well over $1 million—with many people continuing to search for solutions.

The Mission District, for at least the twelfth time in the last 150 years, is in the midst of yet another drastic upheaval. Where it will end is anyone's guess, though it is very likely that today's newcomers will be in for an entirely new set of changes by the year 2030 or so, since major neighborhood transitions seem to have occurred on a fairly regular basis at least since the beginning of European settlement in 1776.

Selected References

Alumni Publications

Alumni Notes (St. Cecilia School)
Future Magazine (Archbishop Riordan High School)
Genesis (St. Ignatius College Preparatory)
George Washington High School Alumni Association Newsletter
Life Anchored in Mercy (alumnae newsletter, Mercy High School)
Lincoln Log (Abraham Lincoln High School)
Lowell Alumni Association Newsletter
Perennial Parrott (Polytechnic High School)
SF State Magazine (San Francisco State University)
SHC Magazine (Sacred Heart Cathedral Preparatory)
USF Magazine (University of San Francisco)

Archives

California Historical Society
Chronicle Vault Photo Archives
Department Store Museum
LGBT Archives
Mission Dolores Archives
OpenSFHistory

Prelinger Archives
Roman Catholic Archdiocesan Archives
San Francisco History Center, San Francisco Public Library
San Francisco Municipal Transportation Association Archives
San Francisco Roman Catholic Archdiocesan Archives
St. Ignatius College Preparatory Photo Archives
Western Neighborhoods Project

Books

Burk, Mary, and Adah Bakalinsky, *Stairway Walks in San Francisco: The Joy of Urban Exploring*. Birmingham, AL: Wilderness Press, 2018.

Caen, Herb. *The World of Herb Caen: San Francisco, 1938–1997*. San Francisco: Chronicle Books, 1997.

Cole, Tom. *A Short History of San Francisco*. Berkeley, CA: Heyday Books, 2014.

Donovan, Diane C. *San Francisco Relocated*. Charleston, SC: Arcadia Publishing, 2015.

Dunnigan, Frank. *San Francisco's St. Cecilia Parish: A History*. Charleston, SC: The History Press, 2017.

Evanosky, Dennis, and Eric J. Kos. *Lost San Francisco*. London: Pavilion Books, 2011.

Garibaldi, Rayna, and Bernadette C. Hooper. *San Francisco Catholics*. Charleston, SC: Arcadia Publishing, 2008.

Hansen, Glady, and Emmet Condon. *Denial of Disaster*. San Francisco: Cameron Books, 1989.

Hitz, Anne Evers. *Emporium Department Store*. Charleston, SC: Arcadia Publishing, 2014.

Hooper, Bernadette C. *San Francisco's Mission District*. Charleston, SC: Arcadia Publishing, 2006.

Kamiya, Gary. *Cool Gray City of Love: 49 Views of San Francisco*. New York: Bloomsbury, 2013.

Koch, Glenn D. *San Francisco Golden Age Postcards*. Sausalito, CA: Windgate Press, 2001.

Lyon, Fred. *San Francisco: San Francisco: Portrait of a City, 1940–1960*. New York: Princeton Architectural Press, 2014.

Martini, John Arturo. *Sutro's Glass Palace: The Story of Sutro Baths*. Bodega Bay, CA: Hole in the Head Press, 2013.

McGloin, John B., S.J. *San Francisco: The Story of a City*. San Rafael, CA: Presidio Press, 1979.

Richards, Rand. *Historic San Francisco*. Lafayette, CA: Great West Books, 2011.

Smith, James R. *San Francisco's Playland at the Beach: The Golden Years*. Fresno, CA: Craven Street Books, 2013.

Solnit, Rebecca. *Infinite City: A San Francisco Atlas*. Berkeley: University of California Press, 2011.

Talbot, David. *Season of the Witch*: Enchantment, Terror, and Deliverance in the City of Love. New York: Free Press, 2012.

Tillmany, Jack. *Theatres of San Francisco*. Charleston, SC: Arcadia Publishing, 2005.

Toland, Jim. *Fog & Fire*. San Francisco: Rico Press, 2014.

Ungaretti, Lorri. *Stories in the Sand: San Francisco's Sunset District, 1847–1964*. San Francisco: Balangero Books, 2012.

Wong, Edmund S. *Growing Up in San Francisco's Chinatown: Boomer Memories From Egg Rolls to Apple Pie*. Charleston, SC: The History Press, 2018

Websites

City and County of San Francisco (sf.gov)
Congregation Emanu-El (www.emanuelsf.org)
Congregation Sherith Israel (www.sherithisrael.org)
Jewish Community Center (www.jccsf.org)
Lick-Wilmerding High School (www.lwhs.org)
Lowell High School (www.lowell.k12.ma.us/lowelllhs)
Nihonmachi Street Fair (www.nihonmachistreetfair.org)
Presidio Trust (www.presidio.gov)
Sacred Heart Cathedral Preparatory (www.shcp.edu)
San Francisco Fire Department (sf-fire.org)
San Francisco Italian Athletic Club (www.sfiac.org)
San Francisco Recreation and Park Department (sfrecpark.org)
San Francisco Unified School District (www.sfusd.edu)
San Francisco Zoo (www.sfzoo.org)
Town School for Boys (www.townschool.com)
United Irish Cultural Center of San Francisco (irishcentersf.org)
West Portal Merchants Association (westportalsf.com)
Wikipedia (www.wikipedia.org)

Magazines and Newspapers

Catholic San Francisco
J. [Jewish News Weekly]
National Geographic
New York Times
San Francisco Chronicle
San Francisco Examiner
San Francisco News-Call Bulletin
San Mateo Times
Westside Observer

Other Works

Brandi, Richard, and Woody LaBounty. *San Francisco's Parkside District, 1905–1957.* Historical Context Statement, San Francisco Mayor's Office, 2007.

Echeverria, Emiliano, et al. *San Francisco's Transportation Octopus: The Market Street Railway* (electronic manuscript). San Francisco: Market Street Railway, 2017.

Rosenberg, Paul. *A Madcap Romp Through San Francisco Politics.* Text of speech, San Francisco, 2011.

About the Author

Author Frank Dunnigan was born in San Francisco during the baby boom years of the 1950s and spent most of his life in the sometimes-foggy Western Neighborhoods. Frank is a graduate of St. Cecilia School, St. Ignatius College Prep and the University of San Francisco. This is his fourth book chronicling local history.

Author's collection.

Triangular steel "dog tag" worn by schoolchildren in the 1950s. *Author's collection.*

Books and Columns by Frank Dunnigan

Classic San Francisco: From Ocean Beach to Mission Bay (2019)

Growing Up in San Francisco: More Boomer Memories from Playland to Candlestick Park (The History Press, 2016)

Growing Up in San Francisco's Western Neighborhoods: Boomer Memories from Kezar Stadium to Zim's Hamburgers (The History Press, 2014)

San Francisco's St. Cecilia Parish: A History (The History Press, 2016)

"Streetwise," a monthly history column published online by Western Neighborhoods Project since 2009 (http://www.outsidelands.org/Author/Frank+Dunnigan)

Opposite: The Claus Spreckels (or Call) Building was an early skyscraper built in 1898 at the corner of 3rd and Market Streets. It burned but remained standing in 1906 and was soon restored. In 1938, its classic dome was removed, and the building was remodeled into a modern style and renamed Central Tower. *Glenn D. Koch collection.*

Souvenir of San Francisco, Cal.

In remembrance of San Francisco.

Visit us at
www.historypress.com